Listening to Your Donors

Listening to Your Donors

The Nonprofit's Practical Guide to Designing and Conducting Surveys That:

- Improve Communication with Donors
- Refine Marketing Methods
- Make Fundraising Appeals More Effective
- Increase Your Income

Bruce Campbell

JOSSEY-BASS
A Wiley Company
San Francisco

Jossey-Bass books and products are available through most bookstores. To contact Jossey-Bass directly, call (888) 378-2537, fax to (800) 605-2665, or visit our website at www.josseybass.com.

Substantial discounts on bulk quantities of Jossey-Bass books are available to corporations, professional associations, and other organizations. For details and discount information, contact the special sales department at Jossey-Bass.

 Manufactured in the United States of America on Lyons Falls Turin Book. This paper is acid-free and 100 percent totally chlorine-free.

The material on focus groups in Resource D was adapted from B. Campbell, "Focus on the Heart of Your Donor," *Fund Raising Management,* June 1996, p. 12. Reprinted with permission.

Library of Congress Cataloging-in-Publication Data

Campbell, Bruce (Bruce Alan), date.
    Listening to your donors : the nonprofit's practical guide to designing and conducting surveys that improve communication with donors, refine marketing methods, make fundraising appeals more effective, increase your income / Bruce Campbell. — 1st ed.
      p. cm. — (The Jossey-Bass nonprofit and public management series)
    Includes index.
    ISBN 0-7879-5037-8
    1. Nonprofit organizations — Finance. 2. Fund raising. I. Title. II. Series.
HG4027.65 .C36 2000
001.4'33 — dc21
                                      00-009795

HB Printing   10 9 8 7 6 5 4 3 2 1   FIRST EDITION

The Jossey-Bass
Nonprofit and Public Management Series

Contents

Figures, Tables, and Exhibits   xi

Preface   xiii

The Author   xvii

Introduction: How Nonprofits Can Improve
    Donor Bonding and Increase Income
    Through Market Research   1

1.   Understanding the Many Different Ways
      to Listen to Your Donors   11

2.   An Overview of the Survey Process   18

3.   Designing Survey Research   28

4.   Designing the Questionnaire   49

5.   Designing Individual Questions   71

6.   Putting It All Together   81

7.   Administering the Survey   109

8.   Analyzing the Survey Results   122

9. Preparing an Effective Survey Report 136

Conclusion 151

Resource A: Glossary 155

Resource B: Exploring Advanced Analyses and
What They Can Do for Your Nonprofit 161

Resource C: When and How to Use
a Professional Researcher 179

Resource D: The Nonprofit Researcher's Toolkit 187

Resource E: Organizations Helpful to
Nonprofit Researchers 207

Index 211

Figures, Tables, and Exhibits

Figures

2.1	Sample Mail Survey Time Line	26
2.2	Sample Telephone Survey Time Line	27
8.1	Pie Graph	133
8.2	Bar Graph	133
8.3	Stacked Bar Graph	134
8.4	Line Graph	135
B.1	Sample Perceptual Map	169
B.2	Sample Perceptual Map with Preferences	170
B.3	Stated Importance of Attributes Versus Actual Influence on Giving	176
D.1	Sample Results of a Factorial-Based Comparison	196
D.2	ABC Nonprofit's Lifetime Donor Values by Source	198
D.3	ABC Nonprofit's Lifetime Value–Lifetime Cost Ratios by Source	199

Tables

3.1	Sample Sizes for Populations over 100,000	45
3.2	Sample Sizes for Smaller Populations	45
8.1	Frequency Analysis for One Question	125

8.2	Confidence Intervals for Specific Survey Responses	127
8.3	Cross-Tabulation Analysis	128
8.4	Banner Analysis	129
B.1	Possible Impact of Ratings Improvement	177
D.1	ABC Nonprofit's Evaluation of Donor Sources Using Lifetime Value	199
D.2	XYZ Organization's Lifetime Value–Lifetime Cost Ratios	201
D.3	Fundraising Overview Report	203

Exhibits

2.1	Sample Mail Survey Budget	23
2.2	Sample Telephone Survey Budget	25
4.1	Sample Introduction to a Blind Telephone Survey	53
4.2	Sample Introduction to a Mail Survey	53
6.1	ABC Health Charity Telephone Questionnaire for Constituents	82
6.2	Beautiful Botanic Garden Mail Questionnaire for Members	98
9.1	University College Research Results	142
9.2	Metro Zoo Research Results	144
9.3	Survey Report Executive Summary	147
9.4	Survey Report Title Page	149
B.1	XYZ Wildlife Society Prospect Profile	166

Preface

For years the for-profit sector has recognized the importance of marketing research, and it has benefited greatly from its use. In recent years nonprofits have also begun to make increased use of marketing research, also referred to as communications or fundraising research. After all, whether they refer to those they serve as donors, members, or constituents, nonprofits also seek to communicate, motivate, and appeal to millions of "customers." One indication of nonprofits' growing interest in research is that my colleagues and I at Campbell Research have seen our business multiply fourfold in the last four years.

With their increasing interest in research, nonprofit executives will find much to benefit from in this book, which provides an overview of marketing research techniques and then focuses in on the most popular method of conducting this research: surveys. Moreover, although there are many good textbooks on survey research, I am not aware of a single volume that is directed toward helping the nonprofit executive with this job. This book was written to fill this gap.

It is also intended to motivate nonprofits to take advantage of the research tools available to them. It describes how research has already helped a number of nonprofits to achieve their goals. It provides step-by-step instructions so that nonprofit executives can design and conduct research with the aid of examples tailored to their needs. Finally, it places survey research in the context of several other types of research beneficial to the nonprofit sector.

Audience

This book is intended primarily for nonprofit executives who must design or oversee fundraising and member research, whether it is performed in house or by a marketing research firm. It will also be very informative for nonprofit executives who use this research, helping them to understand the meaning of the various results and to use these findings appropriately, and for other staff who assist with or apply this research. Finally, this material will broaden the understanding of all nonprofit communications, public relations, and marketing executives who oversee or read research.

Overview of the Contents

The Introduction presents three case histories that illustrate how research helped a small nonprofit, a medium-sized college, and a large national nonprofit.

The first two chapters offer overviews that can assist decision making. Chapter One describes the major forms of marketing research and how they apply to nonprofit organizations. Chapter Two provides an overview of the survey process as well as a sample budget and time line for each of the two major survey methods: mail and telephone.

The next four chapters address preparing the survey itself. Chapter Three outlines instructions for designing a survey project, including suggestions on how to develop a sample, how to set sample size, and how to decide which method to use (for example, telephone, mail, Internet, and so forth). Chapter Four shares specific principles and steps that are important in designing a questionnaire that produces valid results. Chapter Five outlines the steps in designing individual survey questions. And Chapter Six exemplifies how the principles and steps discussed so far can be implemented. It presents two sample questionnaires, a mail survey and a phone survey.

The final three chapters take you through the implementation steps. Chapter Seven explains how to administer the survey either by phone or mail. Chapter Eight describes how to best analyze survey results using statistics and graphs. And Chapter Nine suggests how survey results can be effectively reported.

The Conclusion reviews the critical information this book has equipped you to obtain, information that can help your organization move to a new level of fundraising and communication and achievements.

This book also offers four rich resources. Resource A is a glossary of useful terms. Resource B explores some advanced analyses of survey results and the ways they can be helpful for your nonprofit. Resource C offers ways to help you decide whether it is better for your organization to *make* or *buy* the survey. Resource D is a toolkit containing brief descriptions of several other types of research your nonprofit might find extremely helpful as it seeks to learn about its donors and other constituents.

Acknowledgments

I am grateful for the support of many people while I wrote this book. Dorothy Hearst of Jossey-Bass provided much valuable counsel and encouragement; Jim McGee, Gary Stanton, Tom Clagett, and Jennifer Spencer helped proofread and edit it; Kathie Gonzales and Debby Richards provided administrative assistance; Dirk Rinker, Dan Chrystal, and Tania Chrystal helped lighten my workload in order that I might have more time to write; Wendy, my beloved wife, provided extra writing time by cheerfully caring for our children on Saturdays; Wendy Fischer of Mailworks provided a good sample of a mail questionnaire; Bill Tippie of Bentz Whaley Flessner counseled me regarding prospect research. Most of all, I am grateful to God, without whom I would not be able to take even a breath.

Santa Maria, California   Bruce Campbell
May 2000

To my beloved wife, Wendy,
and our God-sent blessings:
Ruth, Mary, David, Deliverance,
Daniel, John, and James.

The Author

Bruce Campbell is president of Campbell Research, which he founded in 1991. For the eight years before that, as manager of marketing research for World Vision, he played a pivotal role in developing the Marketing Research Division into what many consider to be one of the most advanced marketing research groups in the not-for-profit sector. This division was considered a significant factor in World Vision's doubling its income from $108 million to $215 million during the same period.

Campbell Research clients, both direct and via agencies, have included the American Bible Society, the American Red Cross, the Boy Scouts of America, CARE, the Christian Children's Fund, Food for the Hungry, the Jewish National Fund, the Jewish National Medical Research Center, the Museum of New Mexico Foundation, the National Easter Seals Society, the Prison Fellowship, Project Hope, the Salvation Army, the Urban Alternative, World Vision, the Wycliffe Bible Translators, and many more.

Campbell has repeatedly received national recognition for his work. His marketing and research articles have been published in *Fundraising Management* magazine and in the journals of such national professional associations as the Christian Management Association, National Religious Broadcasters, and the Direct Marketing Association. He has been a featured speaker at national professional association conferences, including those of the National Society of

Fund Raising Executives, the National Catholic Development, the Direct Marketing Association, and the Christian Stewardship Association.

He earned an M.B.A. degree at the UCLA Graduate School of Management and a B.S. degree in economics and psychology at Allegheny College. He maintains a Web site at www.campbell-research.com that includes a great deal of information on survey techniques.

Listening to Your Donors

Introduction: How Nonprofits Can Improve Donor Bonding and Increase Income Through Market Research

We are living in the information age. Now and for the foreseeable future, people will make their fortunes by using information. More specifically, for nonprofit communicators, marketers, and fundraisers, the future is in gathering and using intelligence—marketing and fundraising intelligence.

The nations of the world all have some type of intelligence-gathering system. The largest and most successful for-profit and nonprofit organizations conduct extensive market research. They believe wholeheartedly in information-gathering research. They conduct research frequently and use their findings to enhance their communications, marketing, and fundraising programs accordingly. Intelligence is critical to the health of a nation and of its institutions, and it is just as critical to the health of your organization's communication efforts.

Based on two decades of research experience, this book will prepare you to discover actionable information about your organization's donors and members. Once you know how your constituents feel about your organization, you may discover how to take your organization to a new level of constituent funding, participation, and support.

To give you a sense of the value of research, I will share three stories about nonprofit executives who used research to improve their organizations' standing and strengthen their impact upon humanity. Only their names and some details of their circumstances have been changed, for the purpose of confidentiality. While reading these accounts, think how your organization could benefit if it had the type of information about its constituents that these organizations do.

Pat Turns Around His Organization's Funding

Pat, a former IBM marketing executive and currently the director of marketing for ReUrb, an urban renewal organization, retained one of the finest and most expensive fundraising agencies in the Northeast. Yet the performance of ReUrb's mail appeals was mediocre. Pat wondered whether he should cancel the agency account. Was a direct marketing agency even appropriate for his type of organization? Why were the appeal results so dismal? Did the agency really understand who the donors were and what motivated them? For that matter, Pat wondered to himself, did he as the director of marketing understand who his donors were?

Pat confronted the agency about the lack of results, and the agency representative suggested that ReUrb conduct a donor survey before deciding whether or not to discontinue the agency's services. Pat was trying to decipher the motives behind this request when he remembered his own experience at IBM. The various types of survey research he had helped conduct there had resulted in increased profits. When he had come on board with ReUrb, he had been given only a general feeling about its supporters. A donor survey would indeed provide a much more accurate picture.

When Pat was convinced that a donor survey would maximize ReUrb's income opportunities, he presented the idea to the staff. He was not prepared for their reaction. After all, his experience came from work in the for-profit sector—IBM, no less! He and his former colleagues had taken for granted the cost and the value of research. Any high-tech company that did not invest in research one year was headed toward the financial basement the following year. Marketing research was not a luxury; it was accurate information, and information is power.

Pat's staff consisted of caring people—sincere but inexperienced when it came to the world of marketing. Many had joined the organization out of altruistic motives. Their attitude was summed up by the person who said, "Research? Why should we spend $15,500 for that? We are in the business of helping people. We have gotten this far without research, why should we do it now?" So it took some persuasion, but Pat got the research started.

When the results were in, it was as if a whole new world opened up. For example, contrary to what Pat had been told when he joined ReUrb, the donors were not virtually all African Americans. He had never questioned this assumption before because it seemed right. After all, the famous founder and CEO of the organization (and author of many books) was himself African American and very popular among African Americans. However, the research revealed that almost two-thirds (63 percent) of the organization's donors were Caucasian! Partially validating the staff's original assumption, the research revealed that African Americans did represent 36 percent of the nonprofit's donors, which is three times the percentage of African Americans found in the U.S. population generally. Furthermore, although the typical U.S. charity's African American donors make up only 5 percent of the charity's total donor file, ReUrb, at 36 percent, enjoyed seven times as many. Nevertheless, Caucasians represented almost two-thirds of its file. Pat's eyes were opened to the fact that ReUrb's communications needed to be revamped so that they would appeal strongly to Caucasians as well as to African Americans.

Another revelation came when he learned that half of the donors lived in the suburbs and rural areas; they did not all live in large cities as he had been told. All ReUrb's prior communications had been oriented toward urban dwellers. After seeing the survey results, Pat wondered how many suburban and rural constituents had been hindered or even alienated from supporting ReUrb!

After the staff reviewed the summary research report and held several strategy sessions, they undertook a comprehensive redesign of their appeals and marketing materials. Just one month after the first phase was implemented, this $2 million organization raised enough additional funding to recover the cost of the research. The average gift increased 22 percent, and mailing costs decreased 36 percent. Pat was ecstatic. Later that year he shared his story at several national fundraising conferences. The year after that he was promoted to executive director of the organization.

Sarah Brings Major Donor Giving to a New Level

Sarah, the director of development at Normal College, decided to try a research program to identify the prospects who might become large donors. She had talked with a reputable research and consulting firm about the firm's ability to identify people of wealth in an organization's database by matching that database against a number of national databases. Indicators of wealth such as the value of a person's house; the size of the mortgage; estimated income; auto, boat, or plane ownership; stock transactions; and so on are appended to the nonprofit's database. Using these data and the giving histories contained in the organization's data, and with the help of a mathematical model, the firm can determine which donors and prospects on the file have the greatest capacity to give.

During the second and last phase of the project, the one thousand highest-ranking constituents receive a letter from the organization's CEO or president, letting them know that they will receive a survey call because the organization is interested in learning their wishes for the organization's future and would also like to get to know them better. The survey call helps the organization learn how interested the constituents are in making a major gift, what specific project or purpose might best motivate such a gift, and how much each individual might be willing to give. That information is then used in conjunction with the appended wealth and giving history data to prioritize the prospects by the likelihood that each will make a large gift. Further, an information sheet for each of the one thousand persons surveyed is provided to the organization for follow-up purposes.

Sarah authorized this research and found it to be very helpful for managing her work. She found that a prioritized list of donor prospects provided a framework for turning the large, shapeless goal of making solicitation calls into a concrete, ordered list of tasks. It helped her know not only who should be contacted but who should be contacted *first*.

The list also helped Sarah and her staff to avoid distractions. They needed to make the most of the time they spent generating income for Normal College. Spending time with potential donors was critical, but it had to be coordinated with a host of other responsibilities—attending meetings, coordinating events, developing communications, training volunteers, and so on. Prospect calls are easy to avoid, and there are always temptations to do something else. The prioritized list enabled Sarah's staff to plan their calls more effectively and to resist the temptation to get caught up in less productive tasks.

Not surprisingly, the college was able to raise significantly more money after conducting this research than it had before.

Tom Keeps His National Health Charity on Target

Tom, the vice president of marketing for Puttman National Health, one of the nation's largest medical charities, was responsible for raising $25 million a year. A large goal like that seemed to justify collecting a large amount of marketing intelligence, so Tom was considering investing in research to learn the demographic characteristics of the organization's donors and what they were thinking.

Several years prior to this, Puttman had commissioned a survey from a for-profit sector research firm. While presenting this firm's findings, the senior researcher had pointed out that only a "very small portion of the donor file," 15 percent, would be interested in participating in a monthly giving program. The researcher recommended that this program not even be tested due to the small expected response. But Tom's heart leapt. Fifteen percent! Why, that was terrific! If even half of this group signed up, it would provide a great boost to Puttman's income. Obviously, as good as this research firm may have been in the for-profit sector, it had not understood the nonprofit market or direct-response fundraising in particular.

Tom hired a firm that specialized in fundraising research and understood his organization. He invested $47,000 in research to better understand Puttman's donors and prospects—a large amount but still a small fraction of Puttman's income. The investment was well worth it; what the new research found was traumatic.

The donors had many good things to say about the charity and its communications, but they had also expressed a profound sense of distrust, skepticism, and even fear of being ripped off and deceived! Tom had watched the donors and prospects through the one-way glass of a focus group observation room. Most of them were senior citizens. (The survey results had revealed the average donor was sixty-eight years old.) These donors and prospects shared a similar source for their mistrust. They told the focus group researcher they had grown up believing in and trusting Puttman and other large health and medical charities, just as their parents did. But recent events had made them very concerned that their donations might not be reaching the donors' intended purpose.

The donors in the focus groups recited example after example of nonprofits that were plagued with scandal, that abused their donors, or that had been ripped off by embezzling executives. They never mentioned Puttman, but it was obvious that the same cynicism felt toward the offending institutions spilled over onto the entire nonprofit community.

The researcher, being alert to the importance of this skepticism, asked the donors what information they would need to be assured that their funds were being well spent. She also gathered other intelligence that would later be used to overhaul Puttman's communications strategy.

A bigger shock was the intense reaction against the charity's sweepstakes appeals. This was surprising because Puttman had used sweeps for many years. Tom knew a few people would object to them, but he thought that overall he would hear a positive response, especially considering that the technique was used by other reputable charities. Yet only 20 percent of the focus group participants said they liked the sweepstakes. Another 20 percent did not have a strong feeling one way or the other, but the remaining 60 percent were emphatically opposed to the method. They made comments like, "What is this famous, honorable charity doing in the gambling business?!" and, "How can it be right for many thousands of donated dollars to be given to another donor and not the people in need?!"

This reaction was later confirmed in a telephone survey. Out of the eighteen aspects of Puttman's communications that this survey covered, the sweepstakes' appeal received the most negative ratings. Tom and his staff used this valuable information to fundamentally alter the sweepstakes strategy. Instead of sending the sweepstakes appeal multiple times each year to the whole file, they decided to target a segment of donors identified by the survey and by its giving response history as being favorable to this kind of appeal. The appeal was not sent to donor segments that had been found to think negatively of the sweepstakes.

It was not easy to deal with the research results, but Tom was very pleased that he had conducted the research and faced the results squarely. What he found out was more than how to maximize return on an appeal. He was also able to identify a communications issue, the sweeps appeal, that was harming the organization's image and affecting overall attitudes toward giving.

After this issue was addressed, Puttman's income went up, and Tom was recognized by several nonprofit associations for the excellent work he had performed.

The Moral of the Stories

These are just three examples of how nonprofit marketing and fundraising executives made major, income-producing changes as a result of thorough research. Pat needed to know who his donors were so he could communicate more effectively with them. Sarah needed to distinguish among the giving potentials of many prospects to make better use of her staff's time. Tom needed to know how his organization's communications were affecting its image. In all three cases the knowledge that was gained enabled decisions that led to increased income.

Like Pat, some people use research to help solve problems (his mediocre mail appeals). Others, like Sarah, use research to clarify issues and determine priorities (which prospects to contact). Still other people are like Tom—using research to identify issues and opportunities that otherwise would go unnoticed (credibility concerns and the use of sweepstakes). There are many other good reasons for not-for-profit organizations to use research to listen to their donors and other constituents. One of the best is simply acknowledging that donors are valuable and worth listening to.

Each organization has a unique mission to accomplish and different donors or constituents. Therefore, each one must find out what its own donors are saying. Clearly, one of the best and most time-honored ways to do this is by conducting survey research.

Possibly the greatest proponent of survey research and all forms of marketing research is the for-profit sector. The motives behind this sector's interest in research are straightforward. Research works. More specifically, when properly acted on, it makes a lot of money. The knowledge that comes from finding out what people think of your organization and how they feel you can best serve them, when acted on, is just plain profitable. For organizations of all types, it results in

- More satisfied donors or customers, because they are getting what they want

- Less expensive and more efficient products and services, because the organization is not wasting money on programs, services, or products that are less effective and efficient at helping people

- Happier employees, because they see that the organization cares enough for its constituents to ask how they feel

- More satisfied donors or customers, because the organization is communicating with them in the ways and on the topics that are most meaningful to them

- More funding, because research enables more relevant and motivating communications between the organization and all stakeholders

In the chapters that follow, this book explains how to obtain accurate and actionable survey results so that you can bring your organization to a greater level of service, donor satisfaction, and funding. First, it provides an overview of the types of research available (Chapter One) and the role that survey research plays (Chapter Two). Then it discusses in detail the specific steps required to conduct the research (Chapters Three through Nine). Finally, it offers a bonus, four resources that present a glossary, advanced techniques for analyzing survey results, the points to consider when deciding whether or not to use a professional researcher, and descriptions of additional research techniques.

1

Understanding the Many Different Ways to Listen to Your Donors

Whether they are fundraising, improving public relations, or marketing new products and services, nonprofits need to communicate. However, they can design successful communications only if they have an awareness of who their audience is and how that audience perceives the *message* being delivered, the *medium* through which the message is delivered, and the *messenger* who is delivering it.

In fact, successful communication between a nonprofit and a group of donors or other constituents is very similar to successful communication between individuals. In both cases the connection is greatly enhanced when there is feedback. This feedback allows the initiator to keep the communication relevant and motivating. Without feedback the audience may soon lose interest. Feedback from individuals comes in two forms, verbal and nonverbal, and it is important for organizations to realize that both forms can also be obtained from large groups of people. This chapter outlines the basic ways in which nonprofits can obtain meaningful, accurate, and representative feedback from their donors and constituents.

Verbal Feedback

Nonprofits can obtain three basic categories of verbal feedback from their constituents:

- Constituent-initiated feedback
- Organization-initiated quantitative feedback
- Organization-initiated qualitative feedback

Constituent-Initiated Feedback

Constituent-initiated feedback occurs whenever constituents take it upon themselves to communicate something to the organization. This feedback may take the form of a letter, e-mail, or telephone call. Sometimes it is a compliment; very often it is a complaint or suggestion for improvement. Either way, this feedback can be an occasion for improving the nonprofit's relationship with the specific individual. For example, if an alumna calls to say that her name and address are incorrectly listed in the alumni directory, that feedback helps her university to alleviate a problem. Constituent-initiated feedback is also helpful in raising questions that may need to be the subjects of further research. For example, it may be valuable for the alumna's school to consider whether the error made in her information might also have been made in the information for a number of other alumni. However, in almost all cases it is also critical for organizations to avoid making major or even minor strategic decisions because a few constituents called and expressed a specific concern. Constituent-initiated feedback on any given topic usually comes from less than one-half of one percent of the entire constituent population. What is true for this tiny group is not likely to be valid for the entire population. It is for this reason that scientific surveying methodologies were developed, so that the views of a whole group can be representatively measured.

Organization-Initiated Quantitative Feedback

The most common form of organization-initiated research is the survey. If you were able to conduct a survey involving every one of your constituents (called a *census*), you would know with 100 percent certainty what constituents' attitudes were about a particular topic (assuming their answers were truthful!). However, obtaining feedback from all your constituents (the *population* being studied) would most likely be very expensive, difficult, and time consuming. It would also be unnecessary—you would have a good idea about the attitudes of the whole group long before the census was finished.

Therefore most surveys involve only a small portion of the population (the *sample*). When a survey is conducted correctly, the sample provides feedback that accurately reflects the views of the larger group. The hallmark of a survey is that the results are numerical. Although a survey may not be strong in providing a sense of the depth and quality of constituent feeling, it is great at providing a description of the sample, and thus of the population, in quantified terms. Hence, survey research is often referred to as *quantitative research*.

To ensure that their results are numerically accurate, those conducting surveys must seek to maximize three key factors, *response rate*, *sample size*, and *sample representativeness*. To be useful a survey should have a response rate of 40 percent to 50 percent or better. This ensures that the results reflect the views of the whole group and not just a *self-selected minority* (that is, those who happen to have the time, or perhaps the anger or excitement, to respond), whose opinions are likely atypical of the thoughts of the whole group. Furthermore, a good survey will use a sample sufficiently large to provide a reasonably accurate measure of what the population is feeling. For example, if a nonprofit conducts a survey among a representative sample of six hundred constituents, we know there is a 95 percent chance that the results will be within 4 percent of the result that would come from interviewing the entire constituent population. This rule holds true even for very large groups—as long as the sample is representative of the population.

Quantitative feedback gives nonprofits the ability to numerically quantify an attribute in relation to the whole group, which is especially useful for answering questions like these:

- How many of our constituents think the organization is doing an outstanding job?

- Is our organization's job rating significantly better among major donors than among other donors?

- Has our organization's job rating changed significantly since last year?

Because the hot pursuit of maximizing response rate and sample size almost always prevents surveys from obtaining in-depth information from respondents, researchers must use *qualitative* research to learn about the depth and quality of constituents' thoughts and emotions.

Organization-Initiated Qualitative Feedback

Surveys are of most help when a nonprofit understands exactly what issues it needs to know more about and when the information needed can be framed in easy-to-ask, multiple-choice questions. However, sometimes an organization would like to know what its *donors or constituents* think the issues are. Or maybe it would like to learn how donors feel about complex subjects that cannot be adequately expressed in the simple questions required by a survey. For example, a nonprofit might want answers to these questions:

- How do our constituents decide which organizations to support?

- How would our constituents describe our organization if it were a person; that is, what is our image or personality in their eyes?

- How do our constituents sort through their mail?

To learn this kind of information, nonprofits must use longer interviews with open-ended questions. Qualitative research plays a vital role in helping nonprofits listen to donors because it reveals individuals' more complex thoughts, feelings, and attitudes. This type of interview and the subsequent analysis of answers is very time consuming and not practical with the sample sizes used for valid quantitative research. Because qualitative research deals with smaller and thus less representative groups of donors, its results cannot be assumed to apply to the whole group from which the sample was drawn, and strategic changes should never be based solely on this research. However, one primary strength of qualitative research is that the issues and feelings it reveals can be used to design especially effective surveys for quantitative research, and these surveys can determine the prevalence of these issues and feelings among the whole group.

There are several types of qualitative research, the two most popular being *focus groups* and *depth interviews*. Focus groups are group interviews of eight to ten people, typically lasting about two hours. For organizations whose donors or constituents are regionally or nationally distributed, focus groups are often conducted on weekday evenings in several geographical locations. Focus groups are best held in one of the seven hundred professional facilities located across the United States. (To find one in a particular area, search *The Focus Group Directory* on-line at www.greenbook.org or check the Yellow Pages listings under *market research*.) These facilities have large, attractive meeting rooms, client observation rooms behind one-way mirrors, and audio- and videotaping facilities. To make participants feel comfortable, facility services include a host or hostess who greets the respondent, deals with latecomers, serves refreshments, and distributes the financial incentives that are usually necessary to motivate respondents' attendance.

Due to their inherent group interaction, focus groups are excellent at helping people bring their thoughts and feelings to the surface. Another advantage is that they allow the sponsoring organization's staff to experience in real time the participants' reaction to their questions, either on site or via teleconferencing. Staff also have the opportunity to ask follow-up questions and to videotape the proceedings for future use.

There are also some disadvantages of focus groups to consider. One is that the more vocal participants may dominate the conversation and skew other participants' thinking. However, a trained moderator can largely prevent this from happening. Possibly the main disadvantage is that focus groups require eight to ten people from the target population to convene in one place at one time. This may not be possible when donors or constituents are sparsely distributed geographically. In this case one-on-one depth interviews conducted by phone are the best option.

One-on-one depth interviews are also helpful even though used less than focus groups. They may be the only means of gathering detailed information from a target population that is geographically spread out. Depth interviews are also be preferred when the organization has a strong concern that group interaction might sway some participants' answers or when a topic is so personal that participants would be uncomfortable discussing it in a group.

The disadvantage of depth interviews is that they lack the vital group dynamic found in focus groups. They also require a great deal more interviewer time than focus groups do. For example, interviewing twenty persons for one and one-half hours each requires thirty hours of interviewer time. Conducting two focus groups, each of which lasts two hours and is attended by ten persons, requires only four hours. Also staff are unlikely to have the opportunity to observe interviews or to ask follow-up questions as they can with focus groups.

I am often asked in which order quantitative and qualitative research should be conducted. Although they may be conducted in any order, in my opinion it is usually best to conduct the qualitative research first. The logic here is to start at the more general (open-ended) level of inquiry and move to the more specific. For example, qualitative research may reveal issues and positions on issues that a nonprofit's management may not have thought of previously. These issues can then be investigated further in the survey questionnaire. Yet my preference for preceding quantitative with qualitative research is not a hard-and-fast rule. There are times when it is helpful to conduct focus group research after a survey. For example, a for-profit organization needed to learn which of its twenty new product ideas it should roll out. It conducted a survey to learn which product the customers would be most likely to buy, then it conducted focus groups to learn what features the people likely to buy the product most wanted it to have.

In the situation in which an organization does not have the funds to conduct both qualitative and quantitative research, it is my opinion that the qualitative research should be omitted and the research funds used for a more statistically accurate survey.

Nonverbal Feedback

I have discussed in general how organizations can obtain accurate verbal feedback from their constituents, but what about nonverbal feedback? Some communication experts claim that 70 percent of communication is nonverbal. It is easy to understand what constitutes nonverbal communication between individuals, but what form does this communication take in a group of donors, members, or other nonprofit constituents? Nonverbal feedback encompasses behaviors such as whether constituents give (that is, contribute funds, participate, read, or volunteer), how much they give, how often they give, and to what they give, and it also is found in how these different behaviors are trending over time. Such trends produce especially valuable and actionable feedback. Although the research methods that can accurately identify and interpret these behaviors are not within the scope of this book, Resource D delineates a number of them and presents thumbnail sketches of their purposes and general methodologies.

Conclusion

This chapter has set the stage for market research by nonprofits by discussing the different types of feedback. The next chapter continues this orientation with an overview of the survey process itself.

2

An Overview of the Survey Process

Before getting into the nuts and bolts of conducting surveys, it will be helpful to sketch the major steps involved and suggest what the budgets and time lines might look like.

Action Steps

The typical constituent survey project might follow this chronological course.

Preparing for the Survey

First, the nonprofit makes the decision to conduct market research and sets aside the budget. This budget should be based on the expected value of the information as well as the expected costs. Examples of budgets are shown later in this chapter and guidelines for setting a budget are covered in Chapter Three.

The nonprofit also decides whether to do the research in house or to use a research supplier. The points to consider in this decision are discussed in Resource C. If a supplier is to be used, then candidate firms are identified, proposals are requested and reviewed, and the supplier is selected.

The expected schedule, or time line, for conducting the research is also drafted, taking into account the nonprofit's other activities (such as board meetings, special events, program launch dates) and the availability of the people to be interviewed (Will it be best to survey them on weekdays? Are there holidays to avoid?). Examples of project time lines appear later in this chapter. The time line will also depend on the survey methodology selected, as discussed in Chapter Three.

Next, the nonprofit must put its primary research objective in writing and also its secondary objectives, which are the specific questions it wants answered. This is discussed further in Chapter Three. Just as good travel planning involves selecting a primary destination plus choosing specific things, places, or people to see along the way, so good research project planning must choose its objectives carefully in order to maximize the time and resources invested. Clear objectives maintain focus, help in decision making, assist in prioritizing the information to be collected (and in controlling costs by identifying the most important questions and allowing less important ones to be omitted if necessary), and enable the nonprofit to evaluate and defend the project.

With the survey objectives understood, the nonprofit identifies the population to be studied (for example, regular donors, major donors, or prospects) and determines a method of sampling. The population is the group the research sample should represent. The sampling method determines which specific individuals will be asked for their input as representatives of the population. Sampling issues are discussed in the second half of Chapter Three.

Finally, sample sizes are selected that will provide a balance between the accuracy desired in the results and the cost of performing the survey.

When an outside researcher is used, the steps of setting objectives, identifying the population, and determining sample size are usually performed by the researcher and presented in the research proposal. The researcher may request that the agreement on these matters be put in writing so there will not be any confusion about them later.

Designing the Survey

The next series of steps involves designing the survey. After a questionnaire is drafted, it is reviewed by those involved with or affected by the project. If an outside researcher prepares the questionnaire, it is submitted to the nonprofit for edits and approval. The questionnaire may be made a little longer than the plan calls for so that alternative questions can be considered during the review process.

The reviewers scrutinize the questionnaire to ensure that it will elicit the information desired and that all questions are actionable. Additional drafts may be created and reviewed until all involved are reasonably satisfied.

The next step is to conduct a pretest of the questionnaire by administering it to a small number of people to check whether the questions are clear, whether it can be completed in a reasonable period of time, and whether any other changes should be made. If only superficial changes are needed, they are made, and the survey is implemented. If major changes seem necessary, the revised questionnaire is put through the review process again. Questionnaire design is covered in much more detail in Chapters Four, Five, and Six.

Administering the Survey

The survey is then fielded using the selected methodology (mail, telephone, or the like). Administering surveys is covered in Chapter Seven.

The data are gathered and then entered into an electronic file. Some methodologies allow both steps to occur at once. In others these steps can overlap to some degree, with data entry beginning before data collection is finished. If an outside researcher is handling the data from a mail survey and the completed questionnaires are being returned to the nonprofit, the nonprofit typically sends all the questionnaires it has received so far to the researcher about a week before the cut-off date by which respondents have been asked to return them. The remaining questionnaires are sent along about a week after the cut-off date. This scheduling enables the researcher to begin data entry earlier and provide an analysis of the results sooner.

Analyzing Data and Reporting Results

After the data entry is completed, the data are summarized, described, and analyzed. Implications are drawn, conclusions are reached, and decisions may be recommended. Data analysis is the subject of Chapter Eight. An outside researcher will usually provide a statistical analysis and a conceptual or marketing analysis as part of the final report.

The report should be dated, and it should document the research objectives, the conclusions, the recommendations for current actions, and any topics or issues recommended for future or additional research, organizing and compiling the material into a clear, attractive final document. The writer of the report should be thorough, bearing in mind that someone unfamiliar with the survey may need this information in the future. He or she may have occasional questions to ask during this time. An outside researcher will likely want to know how many final reports are needed. Usually two to four are included in the base survey price. Producing reports is detailed in Chapter Nine.

In most cases, when the report is about one week away from submission, a date is set to present the report to key decision makers and others who may be expected to use or benefit from the results. When the nonprofit is using an outside researcher, this presentation may be the staff's best opportunity to extract maximum value from that researcher's work. All relevant personnel should be gathered for this discussion, and organization leaders may want to wrestle with the implications and possible strategic changes suggested as they come up. Therefore the presenter should plan to be flexible, allowing for this interaction and for brainstorming during the presentation.

Following Up

A year or so later may be a good time for the nonprofit to reevaluate the meaning of the research and any changes that have been made in light of it. In addition, new questions about the results or new issues that might be researched should be discussed. A good research firm may be favorable to returning at that time to discuss these new questions and issues. Following up allows the nonprofit to gain the most from its investment in professional research.

In addition to setting a foundation for learning more about surveys that listen to constituents, this overview description may help a nonprofit decide what it can handle with its internal resources and what it might want to ask an outside firm to handle.

Time and Cost

The time and cost of survey research vary widely, depending upon a number of factors such as the number of populations to be surveyed, the sample size, and the length of the questionnaire. Nevertheless, a typical telephone survey with four hundred responses requires eight weeks, and a mail survey of similar quality will require about fourteen weeks. Sample budgets are displayed in Exhibits 2.1 and 2.2 and sample time lines in Figures 2.1 and 2.2 to give you an initial idea of what is involved. These samples show approximate costs of using an outside researcher. Your total in-house costs will likely be similar if you consider your overhead as well as your out-of-pocket expenses. The examples assume a sample of one thousand people, four hundred of whom respond. Later chapters discuss budgets and schedules further.

Conclusion

The purpose of this chapter has been to provide the reader with an overview of the survey process in terms of action steps, budgets, and time lines. You probably have many questions at this point about implementing the process described here. The remaining chapters will answer these questions in detail.

Exhibit 2.1 Sample Mail Survey Budget.

1. **Initial Costs**
   Meetings with research firm to establish information base
   and prepare a proposal — No charge
   Preparation of preliminary draft questionnaire and
   meeting with researcher to refine questionnaire after
   proposal approval — $1,500
   Selection of respondents, pretest of questionnaire, and
   conducting and preparing final survey instrument — 975 — $2,475

2. **General Costs**
   Mailing list rental (not applicable to donor or member
   survey) — NA
   Nondonor/member mailing list, if necessary[a] — 120
   Typesetting and printing questionnaire (8-page booklet,
   stapled), cover letter, and envelopes (print 1,300 to allow
   for follow-up mailings) — 1,140
   Miscellaneous supplies — 100 — 1,360

3. **First Mailing** (to 800, expecting 50% return)
   Business reply permit with BRMAS (Business Reply Mail
   Accounting System) fee — 300
   Mailing service: folding, collating, stapling, inserting,
   labeling, metering, sorting, bundling: approximate cost
   $100/thousand — 100
   Postage: first-class mail out, 800 @ $.56 (2 oz.), and
   30% replying, 240 @ $.35 — 532
   Tracking respondents and deleting from follow-up mailings — 60
   Management time — 200 — 1,192

4. **Second Mailing** (to 560 nonrespondents to first mailing)
   Postcards — $120
   Printing reminder notice on postcards — 100
   Mailing service: purchase labels, affix to postcards — 75
   Postage: mail out 560 @ $.23, and 10% of initial mailing
   replying, 80 @ $.35 — 157
   Maintaining inventory of respondents — 40
   Management time — 200 — 692

5. **Third Mailing** (to 480 nonrespondents)
   Preparing letter — 150
   Typesetting and printing — 100

Exhibit 2.1 Sample Mail Survey Budget, Cont'd.

Mailing service (see first mailing for details)	75	
Postage: mail out 480 @ $.56, and 10% of initial mailing replying, 80 @ $.35	297	
Maintaining inventory of respondents	20	
Management time	200	842

6. **Data Reduction and Procession**

Cleaning returned questionnaires and postcoding open-ended questions	700	
Computer input	400	
Computer input verification (should achieve 98 percent accuracy)	200	
Computer processing and selection of appropriate statistical output	500	1,800

7. **Data Analysis and Report Preparation**

Analyzing data and preparing report	4,500	
Presentation	750	
Typing, photocopying, binding report	500	5,750

Total Cost	**14,111**

Note: Labor expenses include overhead and payroll tax.

[a]May be higher for a specialized population list not generally available. Additional administrative research may be required.

Source: Adapted from L. M. Rea and R. A. Parker, *Designing and Conducting Survey Research* (2nd ed.) (San Francisco: Jossey-Bass, 1997), pp. 15–16. Copyright © 1997 Jossey-Bass Inc. Reprinted by permission of John Wiley & Sons, Inc.

Exhibit 2.2 Sample Telephone Survey Budget.

1. **Initial Costs**

   Meetings with research firm to establish information base
   and prepare a proposal   No charge

   Preparation of preliminary draft questionnaire and
   meeting with researcher to refine questionnaire after
   proposal approval $1,500

   Selection of respondents, pretest of questionnaire, and
   conducting and preparing final survey instrument: 975 $2,475

2. **General Costs**

   Mailing list rental (not applicable to donor or member
   surveys)   NA

   Typing questionnaire: 100

   Photocopying and stapling questionnaire (6 pages)[a]
   (500 copies to compensate for incomplete interviews)   180

   Miscellaneous supplies   100   380

3. **Recruitment, Selection, and Training of Interviewers**

   Placing recruitment advertisements   50

   Reviewing résumés and scheduling initial review
   of applicants: 80

   Interviewing applicants   200

   Training selected interviewers[b]   270   390

4. **Telephone Interview Process**

   Conducting interviews[c]   3,000

   Conducting follow-up interviews: 5% recalled   200

   Replacement sample selection and supervision: 300

   Telephone charges[d]   400   3,900

5. **Data Reduction and Processing**

   Cleaning returned questionnaires and postcoding
   open-ended questions   700

   Computer input   400

   Computer input verification (should achieve 98 percent
   accuracy)   200

   Computer processing and selection of appropriate
   statistical output   500   1,800

6. **Data Analysis and Report Preparation**

   Analyzing data and preparing report   4,500

   Presentation   750

   Typing, photocopying, binding report   500   5,750

Total Cost   15,025

Note: Labor expenses include overhead and payroll tax.

[a]Note the difference from the mail survey–no cover or return address is necessary.

[b]Assumptions: Six interviewers are selected to complete 400 interviews; each interviewer receives three hours of training in one session; interviewers work a thirty-hour week, completing two questionnaires per hour.

[c]Time may vary based on language issues, screening requirements, and ease of access to respondent population.

[d]Charges may vary considerably based on geographical range of interviews.

Source: Adapted from L. M. Rea and R. A. Parker, *Designing and Conducting Survey Research* (2nd ed.) (San Francisco: Jossey-Bass, 1997), p. 17. Copyright © 1997 Jossey-Bass Inc. Reprinted by permission of John Wiley & Sons, Inc.

Figure 2.1 Sample Mail Survey Time Line.

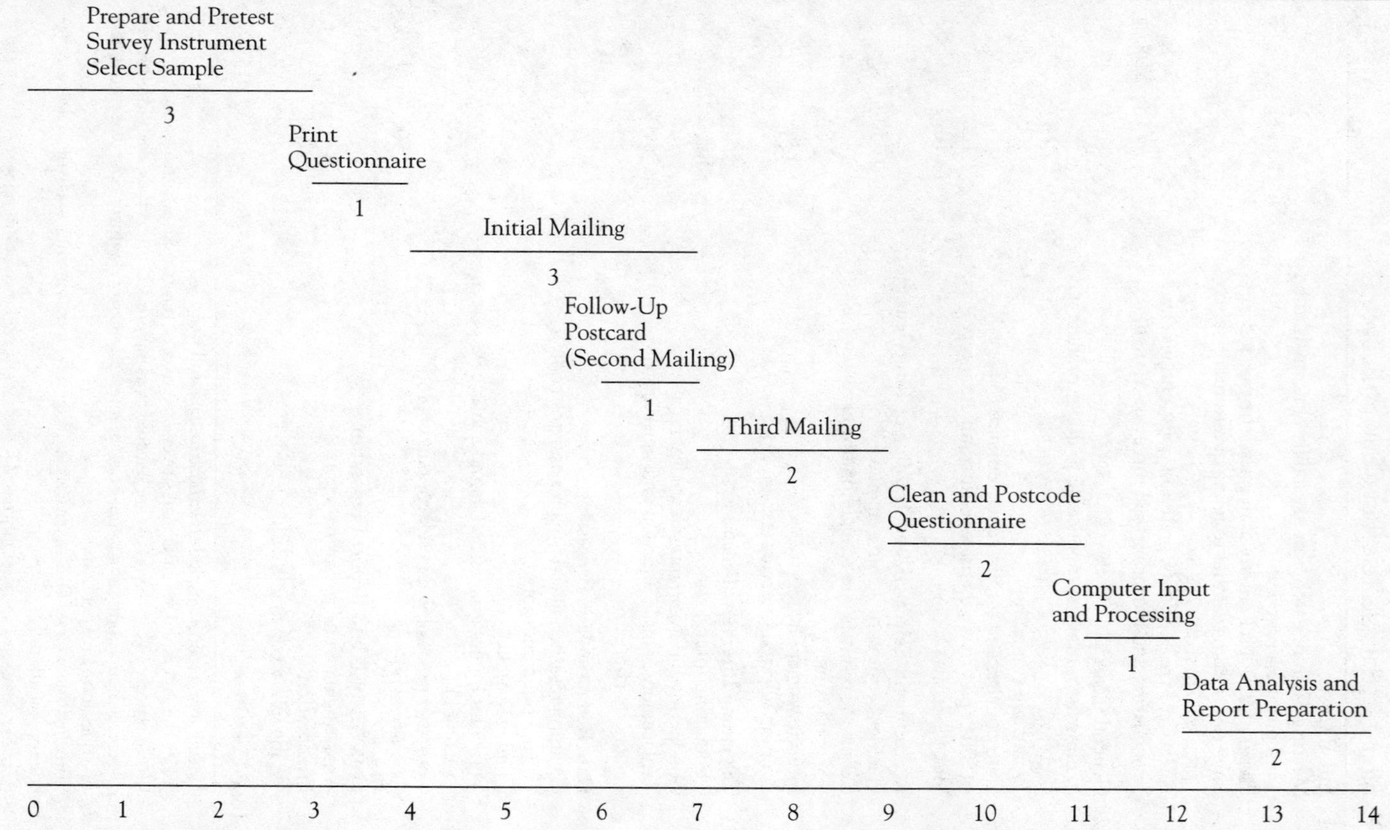

Prepare and Pretest
Survey Instrument
Select Sample

3

Print
Questionnaire

1

Initial Mailing

3

Follow-Up
Postcard
(Second Mailing)

1

Third Mailing

2

Clean and Postcode
Questionnaire

2

Computer Input
and Processing

1

Data Analysis and
Report Preparation

2

0   1   2   3   4   5   6   7   8   9   10   11   12   13   14

Source: L. M. Rea and R. A. Parker, *Designing and Conducting Survey Research* (2nd ed.) (San Francisco: Jossey-Bass, 1997), p. 20. Copyright © 1997 Jossey-Bass Inc. Reprinted by permission of John Wiley & Sons, Inc.

Figure 2.2 Sample Telephone Survey Time Line.

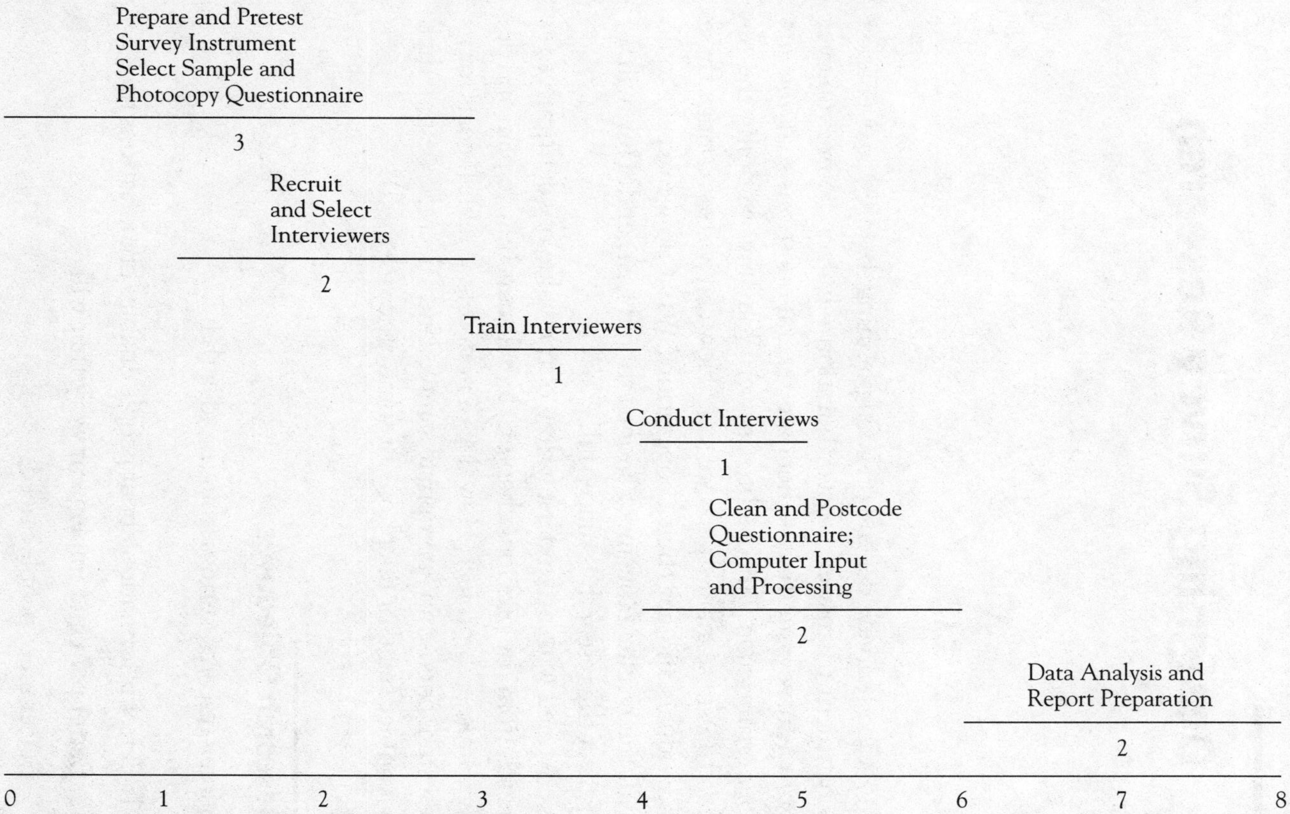

Prepare and Pretest
Survey Instrument
Select Sample and
Photocopy Questionnaire

3

Recruit
and Select
Interviewers

2

Train Interviewers

1

Conduct Interviews

1

Clean and Postcode
Questionnaire;
Computer Input
and Processing

2

Data Analysis and
Report Preparation

2

0   1   2   3   4   5   6   7   8

Source: L. M. Rea and R. A. Parker, Designing and Conducting Survey Research (2nd ed.) (San Francisco: Jossey-Bass, 1997), p. 21. Copyright © 1997 Jossey-Bass Inc. Reprinted by permission of John Wiley & Sons, Inc.

3

Designing Survey Research

Good surveys depend on good planning. Before you ever ask a constituent to answer a survey question—in fact, before you ever write a survey question—there are several questions that *you and your organization* will need to answer: Why are we doing the research? Whose input should we seek? How can we best contact these individuals and get their cooperation? What do we expect to do with the results? How much money should we spend? How will we know if the research is successful?

Armed with an understanding of the value of quantitative research from the previous chapters, let's discuss how to plan and design a research project. How does a nonprofit establish goals for its research, choose an appropriate sample, and select the best method of contact (mail or telephone or some other method)?

Research Objectives

Survey research springs from the idea that

1. Better information about people enables organizations to
2. Better plan and implement work that will
3. Better meet people's needs

The planning for the research can start with any of these three components and should eventually tie all three together. For example, you might start by asking, What information about our constituents would be most useful to us? or, How can we create or adapt events and programs that will involve more people? or, How can we increase gift income in order to reach more people through our programs?

Consider the following action steps, which illustrate responding to the need for information about constituents:

1. Hold a brainstorming session of key staff during which each person describes the types of information that he or she feels would be most useful and helpful to the organization.

2. Have staff identify the constituent groups that would need to be queried to obtain each piece of information mentioned in step 1.

3. Prioritize these constituent groups based on the overall value (that is, the amount and importance) of the information that could be obtained from each one.

4. Given the value of the information that could be obtained from the top-ranked group, determine the maximum you feel it would be worthwhile to spend on research to learn that information. The cost of even the lowest-quality survey is almost always at least $5,000. Therefore, if the information is not worth at least $5,000, your organization probably should not pursue the research. Instead, organizational leaders should rely on their experience and intuition to make the necessary decisions. If the information is worth researching, establish a budget to research this constituent group, keeping in mind that the budget should be commensurate with the value of the information. For example, if you feel the information could help your nonprofit raise $100,000 more per year after expenses, a budget of $5,000 is unlikely to get the most out of

your information-gathering opportunity; a budget of $50,000 might be more appropriate. (Costs are discussed later in this chapter.)

5. Go back to steps three and four and determine what it would be worthwhile to spend on researching the constituent group with the next highest amount and quality of information that the organization needs. Repeat steps 3 and 4 for each constituent group.

Once you have determined the information the organization could gather from each constituent group and whether it would be worthwhile to fund the research to obtain it, it is helpful to put the primary objective and any secondary objectives of the research project into writing. Formally recording these goals carries several benefits. First, it provides a focus for the design of the survey instrument, enabling the designer to write better questions and to make a better choice of questions to cut if the survey needs to be shortened. Second, it helps keep everyone involved reading from the same page from the outset—that is, they start from a point of agreement. One reason this is important is that research information often suggests change, and change frequently calls forth resistance. A common first point of resistance is to question the purpose, value, or credibility of the research. With the primary and secondary goals written out and shared beforehand, the research is much more likely to be understood, accepted, and acted upon. Finally, these written objectives can be a good guide for those who must implement research results.

The Primary Objective

The primary objective is easily obtained by identifying the thread of logic that ties together all of the information needs identified. Here are some examples of primary objectives for a variety of nonprofit research purposes. You might use them as models when you are developing your own goal.

Comprehensive donor survey. The primary objective is to learn who the donors are, including their demographics (that is, age, gender, marital status, number of children, income, and education) and psychographics (that is, lifestyles and values), and to identify their perceptions, attitudes, and motivations in order to improve the nonprofit's communications, service delivery, and donor bonding and ultimately to increase donations.

Comprehensive constituent or member survey. The primary objective is to seek to learn who the constituents or members are demographically and psychographically and to identify their perceptions, attitudes, and motivations. This should increase the nonprofit's ability to improve communications and constituent or member bonding, resulting in increased financial support and longevity of participation.

Prospect survey. The primary objective is to learn who the nonprofit's prospective donors, members, or constituents are demographically and psychographically and to identify which of their perceptions, attitudes, and motivations might increase the nonprofit's ability to cost effectively acquire them as faithful and generous donors, members, or constituents.

Major donor survey. The primary objective is to gather more specific information about each individual on the nonprofit's database—especially the person's general ability to give (for example, her disposable income), the person's inclination to give to this nonprofit specifically, and the programs, services, offers, and gift amounts that would most likely motivate a gift—in order to facilitate personal follow-ups. The secondary objective is to obtain a representative picture of the donor file. (The goal of learning about each donor as an individual means that whereas most surveys question a random sample, the major donor survey is used with the entire donor file or, if it is known, with that portion of the file with the potential for major gifts.)

Readership survey. The primary objective is to learn which people read the nonprofit's publication, how they read it, and what content and format they prefer. This could lead to improved readership and ultimately increased education, as well as to increased donor or constituent participation.

Program effectiveness survey. The primary objective is to learn who the recipients of the nonprofit's services are and their perceptions of, attitudes toward, and experiences with these services, allowing the organization to improve program effectiveness.

These are the surveys and primary goals I have encountered most often in my experience with medium and large nonprofits in the United States. Nonprofits will find they can design other survey types and appropriate primary goals as the need for them arises.

Secondary Objectives

Having defined the primary research objective, it is important to further define the survey results that are desired by delineating supplementary goals. It is from these detailed expectations that specific survey questions can later be designed. Oftentimes these secondary objectives will be virtually identical to the types of information that the nonprofit's staff identified in their initial brainstorming session. Here, for example, is a set of subordinate goals, in question format, for a comprehensive donor survey for an organization I will call ABC Nonprofit:

- What is the vision these donors have for ABC Nonprofit?

- What themes and messages will most motivate them to give?

- What specific projects will most motivate giving, and why?

- What kinds of communications will help these donors to feel bonded with ABC Nonprofit and excited about helping it?

- What level of relationship and commitment are these donors looking for? How can that relationship and commitment be deepened and improved?

- How is ABC Nonprofit perceived by the donors? How can this perception be improved?

- If donors have misperceptions, how can they be corrected?
- What do the donors like best and least about ABC Nonprofit? What do these likes and dislikes suggest about ways to maximize campaign success?
- What aspect of the organization and its campaigns do donors want to learn more about?
- What are the donors' demographics and psychographics?
- How do the answers to these questions differ among the four main donor types: current, lapsed, monthly pledges, and major?
- How do the answers to these questions vary depending on donor gender, age, date of last gift, size of largest gift, frequency of giving, and time on the file (that is, since the first gift)?

Response Rates and Methodologies

To meet your objectives you need valid results. A poor response rate is probably the greatest enemy of validity, and it therefore deserves in-depth attention here so you can design your survey with an eye to achieving a healthy response. One day I received a high-quality glossy magazine, put out by a professional association, that contained the results of the magazine's recent reader survey. I enjoyed perusing the results at first, but after a while I found myself becoming increasingly unsettled. I had spoken at this association's national conference several times and mingled with its professionals. The survey results were not matching up with my general sense of who these people were. My sense was that they did not have an average age of sixty-two, were not almost completely male, and so forth. Was there something wrong with my perceptions or something wrong with the survey, I wondered. Toward the end of the article I got my answer. With no apology the article writer shared the survey's vital statistics. About 5,000 questionnaires had been distributed, but only

140 had been returned. This response rate of 2.8 percent (140 divided by 5,000) was one of the worst I had ever seen! And what was even more worrying than the fact that these results were basically worthless was the lack of evidence that the association saw anything wrong with the results. The association magazine dedicated generous space to the survey and did not suggest that the sample was inadequate. Very likely, association staff assumed the results were accurate and were going to base a major portion of their strategic planning on them!

This example suggests an important principle in nonprofit intelligence gathering: *one thing worse than not knowing your donors is to think you know them when you do not.*

Producing intelligence data is different from building physical commodities. With the latter you usually have a sense of what the product should look like. When you buy it, you can see you are getting the right thing. Better yet, you can test it. Whether it's a toaster, a computer, a chair, or a new roof; you can try it out. If it doesn't toast, compute, support your weight, or keep water out of your home, you know it isn't working. This is not true for survey research. The reason you are conducting the survey is that you don't know what the truth is. If you knew, you wouldn't be performing the research.

Response rate is one of the most critical means of assessing a survey's quality. Response rate is, very simply, the number of completed questionnaires as a percentage of the total number distributed (or, for telephone research, the total number of people contacted).

The expected response rate depends on a number of factors, including the type of respondents being sought, their interest in the subject of the survey, the survey methodology, the time required to complete the survey, whether or not a monetary or other incentive is offered to participants, and what or how much the incentive is. A maker of surgical instruments seeking input from neurosurgeons on new product prototypes will have much more difficulty attracting respondents than will a nonprofit seeking input from its current donors. For surveys among nonprofit constituents—especially donors—a good rule of thumb in the professional research community is to obtain a response rate of 50 percent or better. This level is achievable for nonprofits, and at this level the likelihood is strong that the results reflect the thoughts and feelings of the entire target population and not just those of a self-selected minority. Researchers can increase response rate by various means, including making it easier for the donor to respond (shortening the survey, giving respondents reminder calls or cards, and so forth) and increasing the benefits of responding (offering monetary incentives, a free copy of the survey results, or participation in drawings or giveaways, for example).

Advantages and Disadvantages of Some Different Survey Methodologies

Because the costs of research and the resulting benefits to the nonprofit, and of course the response rate, vary across the different survey methodologies, this section reviews some of them. But I must warn you, I will be telling you that most of these very popular methods of conducting surveys are usually ineffective! I concentrate only on well-designed and -conducted telephone and independent mail surveys in this book because they are the ones I have found most effective.

Enclosing a Survey with a Magazine or Newsletter

Advantages	Disadvantages
Low cost. Convenient.	Usually goes to all publication recipients, far more individuals than necessary.
	Usually generates unacceptable response rates (1% to 10%).

Conclusion. These surveys are possibly not worth the paper they are printed on; the results are likely to be biased and deceptive because of the self-selected minority that responds.

Enclosing a Survey with an Appeal

Advantages	Disadvantages
Possibly low cost, if sent to a sample, not the whole file.	Usually goes to the whole file, far more recipients than necessary.
Possibly convenient.	Usually generates unacceptable response rates (2% to 15%).

Conclusion. This method is unacceptable due to its low response rate and self-selection among respondents. They are usually responding because they are favorably biased toward the nonprofit.

Conducting In-Person Interviews

Advantages	Disadvantages
Can use exhibits or product samples.	May be affected by interview bias.
Effective with geographically concentrated populations, such as event attendees.	Not applicable to geographically dispersed donor populations because the visitation cost is prohibitive.
Usually achieves a high response rate due to personal interaction.	May bias the respondent toward answers that the interviewer is thought to favor.
Can be useful in major donor and prospect surveys, communicating the high value placed on the respondent's opinions.	

Conclusion. This method is effective when an entire or a truly representative target population is located in a single geographical area and is not too large. In such cases the use of computer-mediated interviewing is highly recommended to reduce the favorable bias resulting from personal interaction and to allow question and response rotation as well as automatic data entry. Unfortunately, this method is cost prohibitive in many circumstances.

Surveying on the Internet

Advantages	Disadvantages
Relatively inexpensive.	Currently inadequate for most nonprofit purposes because relatively few constituents access it, whereas 95 percent have phones and mailing addresses.

Conclusion. This method is appropriate only when the survey is asking constituents about their Internet usage, their opinion of Web sites, and so forth.

Conducting an Independent Mail Survey

Advantages	Disadvantages
Can include such visual material as samples, pictures, and text.	Requires a relatively long time to prepare and implement.
Is less intrusive than phoning.	Requires follow-up mailings for acceptable response rate.
Is less expensive than phone surveys for surveying very large samples.	May cost more than phone surveys for samples under 500.

Conclusion. This method usually produces good results if enough follow-up mailings are sent. Because the extra mailings may drive the cost close to or above that of a phone survey, the phone survey is generally preferred by professional researchers.

Conducting a Telephone Survey

Advantages	Disadvantages
Is the quickest method.	May cost more than mail surveys for very large samples.
With computerization, can achieve desired samples and subquotas.	Tends to produce favorably biased responses when the nonprofit itself does the calling.

Usually achieves a higher response rate than any method other than in-person interviews.

With computer-assisted rotation of questions and response options, reduces biased answers.

Conclusion. Telephone surveys produce the best quality results for most applications and are still fairly cost effective.

Employing Hybrid Methods

Sometimes, implementing a combination of survey methodologies can maximize the advantages and minimize the disadvantages of individual methods. An example is the phone-mail strategy. Respondents are first contacted by telephone and asked to participate in the study. Those who agree receive a survey packet in the mail to complete and return. This strategy allows the nonprofit to use visual materials and complex questions that might be difficult to employ in a telephone survey. At the same time it encourages a higher response rate than is likely from a mail survey alone. This hybrid approach is more expensive than a mail survey alone, but it can be the most cost-effective approach if the visual materials have substantial value (as educational curricula might have, for example). An extension of this method is the phone-mail-phone approach, in which responses are collected by telephone after the survey packet is mailed to participants who were qualified in an initial phone call.

Sampling

As important as achieving a good response rate and selecting an appropriate methodology are, there is more to consider to obtain accurate and actionable survey results. You need to plan whom you will sample, how you will sample them, and how many you will sample.

Asking the Right People

One of the most important factors in sampling is asking your questions of the "right" people. Who are these right people? In the science of survey research several concepts have been developed to help us sort these people out. Usually the group that an organization is interested in learning about is referred to as the *universe* or, as I mentioned earlier, the *population*. For example, let's say that a museum wants to learn who its members are demographically and psychographically and to discover their perceptions, attitudes, and motivations regarding the organization. Furthermore, let us assume that the museum can afford to conduct a survey only once every three years. Therefore it would also like to know the same information about any people who may become members in the next three years. This group of members and anticipated members is the population or universe for the survey.

Often it is not possible to survey the entire population. For this reason a *working population* is chosen, a group that is representative of the general population and from which the researcher is likely to be able to obtain a sample of respondents.[1] In the museum example the logical working population is made up of the museum's current members. The *sampling frame* is the actual list of members in the database that will be used to select people to be surveyed. Thus, identifying the best sampling frame for a nonprofit is usually very simple when it comes to current constituents, because they are usually in the organization's database.

However, there are times when it becomes a little more complicated. For example, what if a nonprofit desires to conduct a survey of its prospects? The general population is then defined as all those who might reasonably join or who are worth targeting. The working population might then be those who give to other similar organizations. For example, a New York City botanic garden's working population for prospects might include the current members of

[1]L. M. Rea and R. A. Parker, *Designing and Conducting Survey Research* (2nd ed.) (San Francisco: Jossey-Bass, 1996).

thematically or geographically similar organizations, such as New York–area botanical and horticultural societies and a nearby art museum, and it might also include the people in the garden's geographical area who subscribe to gardening and home decorating magazines. However, the botanic garden may not be able to purchase the membership lists of competing organizations for the purpose of selecting people for survey participation, and it may therefore decide simply to rent the subscriber lists of a few of the gardening publications. These latter lists of names will then become the sampling frame.

Once a nonprofit has identified the general population, the working population, and the sampling frame in which it is interested, its next step is to determine how it will select names from the sampling frame for the actual *sample*.

Deciding How You Should Sample

When your organization is conducting survey research in house, it is usually best in terms of practicality and efficiency to obtain a systematic random sample. This is the procedure used most often by nonprofits, and it is the easiest to implement. The systematic random sample is summarized in the following sections along with various other sampling techniques.

There are two basic categories of sampling strategies, *probability* and *nonprobability*. Probability sampling techniques are those in which the probability of selecting any given member of the sampling frame is equal to the probability of selecting any other member. Nonprobability techniques are those in which the probability of selecting a given member is not known. The probability techniques are the only ones that will provide results that are an accurate reflection of the population, which is usually the goal of the survey. The following three techniques are all probability techniques.

Random Sampling. As its name implies, *random sampling* is designed to be as random as possible. This type of sampling is the equivalent of mixing names in a hat and then asking a blindfolded person to draw a certain number of them. However, often the number of people in the working population is so high that manual name drawing is impractical. Therefore a computer program is usually used. Many spreadsheets and statistical software packages include random number generators that can be used to select a sample. Nonprofits that do not have such software often rely on systematic random sampling.

Systematic Random Sampling. *Systematic random sampling* is especially useful with large populations. It is also referred to as the N*th name select*, because every N*th* name is selected from a list, N being the number that results when the total population is divided by the number of names desired in the sample. For example, if a college has thirty thousand alumni names on its database and only one thousand people are needed for a sample, the database manager might implement a procedure of selecting every thirtieth name. This ensures that the sample is selected evenly from throughout the database.

It is important that the process start at the beginning of the database and end right at the end of it to ensure random results. For example, consider what would happen if the database manager incorrectly estimated the size of the database, thinking it held 30,000 names when it really held 55,000. The sample would be complete when the process had gone only halfway through the database, a result that would greatly increase the likelihood of a skewed sample. If the names on the database have been sorted previously by class year, the sample will include names from only the earlier class years. If the database has been sorted by last name, there might be an unusually high incidence of some surnames and therefore ethnicities and a relative lack of others.

Stratified Random Sampling. Sometimes the working population is composed of mutually exclusive subgroups that warrant separate analysis. For example, let's say a nonprofit wishes to survey its current donors but wants to separate out the results for the major donors, which it defines as individuals whose largest gift ever was $1,000 or more. Furthermore, let's assume that the donor file has thirty thousand donors and one thousand major donors. A random sample of eight hundred persons will yield only about twenty-seven major donors. Samples of one hundred are usually the minimum desirable for a subgroup, so twenty-seven is clearly inadequate. The nonprofit needs to obtain a separate sample of at least one hundred major donors.

Such separation of a sample into groups, or strata, with adequately sized random samples is called *stratified random sampling*. As a result of creating this stratified random sample, however, the overall results will be skewed toward the opinions of the smaller strata. Therefore, to generate accurate overall results, the researcher needs to weight the data so that the data from each subgroup make up a percentage of the results proportionate to the percentage of that group in relation to the whole group. Because of this complication, nonprofits without a qualified staff researcher may find it best to refer any stratified surveys they require to professional firms.

Nonprobability Sampling. As mentioned, a nonprobability sample is one for which the chances of selecting a specific member of the working population are not known, and therefore there is no way to ensure representative sampling. Unfortunately, nonprofits often conduct surveys like this and obtain invalid results without being aware they have done so. For example, a zoo might conduct a member survey at the gate as visitors come in. No one knows the chance that any one member will come in during the day, and therefore the sample is skewed. Another example is the organization that wants to know what people think of a certain event, so its staff set up a survey booth at the event and try to pull in passersby. The results of the survey are not likely to reflect the views of the event attendees in general, only the views of those who have walked near the booth and whose presence may in fact have been influenced by whether a restroom or a snack bar was located nearby. In any case, nonprofit executives are cautioned to identify and avoid using these nonprobability samples in forming any conclusions about their constituents.

Again, when a nonprofit is conducting survey research in house and is not sure which sampling method to use, it is usually best to choose the systematic random sampling method.

Having discussed who to sample and how to sample, let's consider how many to sample.

Selecting an Adequate Sample Size

There is an entire branch of mathematics that pertains to statistical theory. Even as it pertains specifically to sampling, much of this information would not be of practical use to the nonprofit executive and therefore goes beyond the scope of this book. Those issues that are of practical value are summarized here. (Those who wish a deeper understanding of these applications of statistical theory could begin by consulting chapter 6 of Rea and Parker's *Designing and Conducting Surveys*.)

Two concepts in particular are important in understanding the accuracy of results that varying sample sizes can provide: *confidence level* and *estimate of error* (aka *confidence interval*). We have all seen the results of a published survey, such as a poll on who the next president of the United States will be, and noted that the fine print says something like this: "the estimate of error is +/– 3 percent." In other words, if the pollsters had asked the question of everyone in the entire population, that result would likely be within +/– 3 percent of the result for the sample.

I use the word *likely* because the population result would not always fall within the stipulated margin of error. Researchers can choose, by the size of the sample they select, whether the population result would be expected to fall within the margin of error 90 percent of the time, 95 percent of the time, 99 percent of the time, or some other percentage. The percentage adopted is called the *confidence level*. Almost always, confidences levels of 90 percent, 95 percent, or 99 percent are chosen, with 95 percent being the level most used in for-profit market research. A 95 percent level is felt to offer a good balance between the risk of accepting as true results that are in actuality false and the risk of accepting as false results that are in actuality true.

With this basic understanding of these concepts, we can proceed to discussing ways to determine appropriate sample sizes. From here on the discussion will assume that the goal in selecting a sample is always to achieve a 95 percent confidence level.

There are of course mathematical formulas that can be used to determine the margin of error for each proposed sample size and vice versa. The formulas consider the type of statistic being estimated (proportions, means, or the like), the confidence level, and the population size. They also consider the distribution of responses. For proportions, they consider how close each question's expected results are to the extremes (0 percent and 100 percent) or to the midpoint of 50 percent; for means, they consider the dispersion of the results (how spread out or compacted the answers tend to be around the mean).

However, far more convenient to use than the mathematical formulas are sample size tables. Table 3.1 can be used to determine the minimum sample size needed to achieve a given estimate of error when proportions (the percentages of people who give particular responses) are being sought, assuming a large population, that is, more than one hundred thousand. Table 3.2 shows sample sizes for smaller populations, which require somewhat smaller samples than large populations for the same margin of error ranges.

Before a nonprofit can determine an adequate sample size for its survey, the staff need a sense of how accurate the results need to be for their purposes. Generally, a margin of error of +/– 10 percent is the greatest that should be accepted. The smallest margin of error that is desirable is determined by balancing the need for accuracy against the cost of the larger sample that increased accuracy requires. Here are the action steps you can follow to determine which sample size is best for each of the constituent groups you identified as worthwhile to survey.

TABLE 3.1 Sample Sizes for Populations over 100,000.

Confidence Interval (Estimate of Error)	Sample Size
± 1%	9,604
± 2%	2,401
± 3%	1,068
± 4%	601
± 5%	385
± 6%	267
± 7%	196
± 8%	151
± 9%	119
± 10%	97

Note: Assumes a confidence level of 95%.

Source: L. M. Rea and R. A. Parker, *Designing and Conducting Survey Research* (2nd ed.) (San Francisco: Jossey-Bass, 1997), p. 119. Copyright © 1997 Jossey-Bass Inc. Reprinted by permission of John Wiley & Sons, Inc.

TABLE 3.2 Sample Sizes for Smaller Populations.

Population Size	Estimate of Error		
	± 3%	± 5%	± 10%
500	250	218	81
1,000	500	278	88
1,500	624	306	91
2,000	696	323	92
3,000	788	341	94
5,000	880	357	95
10,000	965	370	96
20,000	1,014	377	96
50,000	1,045	382	96
100,000	1,058	383	96

Note: Assumes a confidence level of 95%.

Source: L. M. Rea and R. A. Parker, *Designing and Conducting Survey Research* (2nd ed.) (San Francisco: Jossey-Bass, 1997), p. 121. Copyright © 1997 Jossey-Bass Inc. Reprinted by permission of John Wiley & Sons, Inc.

Action Steps to Determine Sample Size

1. Given the budget your nonprofit has formulated for the research and the staff's determination of the value of the survey information they desire to obtain, look at Table 3.1 to determine the maximum sample the nonprofit can afford.

2. Identify the estimate of error that corresponds to this sample size. If it is more precise than your organization needs, you can save a little money by dropping the sample size to a level that corresponds to the least precise error of estimate with which you are comfortable. For example, let's assume that your organization can afford a sample that corresponds to a margin of error of +/– 4 percent. However, if you realize that results accurate to +/– 5 percent will still permit the nonprofit to make the decisions it needs to make, then you can save money by dropping the sample size to one that corresponds to the +/– 5 percent estimate of error.

3. Use Table 3.2 if your population is under 100,000. It will suggest that your sample does not need to be quite as large as suggested by Table 3.1, and this is likely to save your organization a little money. Note, however, that the sample sizes for all but the smallest populations are generally well within 10 percent of the large population sample sizes for the same margins of error.

In my experience the best sample sizes for nonprofits with populations of five thousand are generally in the two hundred to one thousand range. A small nonprofit (for example, with an annual income between $500,000 and $4 million) conducting a survey of peripheral importance might choose a sample of two hundred. A comprehensive donor survey for a small nonprofit might feature a sample of four hundred, whereas a medium-sized organization (with an income between $4 million and $15 million) might consider a sample of six hundred. Larger organizations would work with larger samples. These survey sizes and costs are calculated with phone surveys in mind. It is often cost effective to increase the sample sizes of mail surveys because the cost of obtaining each *additional* questionnaire is less for mail than for phone surveys.

Mining for Results by Subsampling

Sometimes, as I suggested earlier, a nonprofit needs to divide the sample among specific groups of constituents so that specific results can be obtained for each subgroup as well as for the group as a whole. For example, the director of a drug and alcohol rehabilitation agency required a donor survey that would give him specific results for each of four subgroups: major donors, monthly pledgers, current donors, and lapsed donors. Because he had only enough money to survey a total sample of 400, my firm obtained a sample of 100 per group. In this situation the accuracy of the results for each group was +/– 10 percent (see Table 3.1).

In another case the vice president of direct marketing for one of this nation's largest charities wanted us to conduct a survey of his sweepstakes-acquired donors. Recognizing that there might be significant differences in donors' opinions, depending upon the extent of donor involvement with the organization's sweeps program, he requested a sample of three hundred for each subgroup consisting of newly acquired donors, lapsed donors, or multigift donors, which gave the organization results for each group that were accurate to +/– 5.8 percent. In yet another instance an inner-city rescue mission asked us to subsample prospects by the various geographical regions that received mission appeals. These are just a few examples of the ways surveys can use subsampling to target specific groups of interest, yielding more detailed results.

When nonprofit executives feel they would benefit from obtaining results from specific donor groups, that choice has an impact not only on the sample size chosen but on the way it is chosen. For example, one day we received a call from a Christian ministry that wanted to learn whether a special issue of its magazine was effective. This issue was actually a devotional guide that had been sent to

50,000 nondonors who had requested it after hearing about it on the radio and to 150,000 donors who received the regular issues of the magazine. The nonprofit director felt that he did not need results to be any more accurate than +/– 6 percent to make his decision and therefore that he needed a sample of about 250 per group. However, the number of radio requesters was relatively small, so if we had randomly sampled the complete 200,000-person file, we would have had to call about 1,000 people before interviewing the 250 required radio requesters. This would have been waste of resources. So we drew our 250-person samples from the two groups separately.

In summary, the sample size chosen will depend on the number of subgroups you wish to study and the accuracy of the result you want from each group.

Conclusion

This chapter discusses the importance of (1) deciding the overall sample size needed as well as the size of any subgroup to be surveyed, based on the desired level of accuracy and the available research budget, and (2) choosing a survey methodology that is appropriate for the kinds of results sought, achieves an acceptable response rate, and has an acceptable cost. This information should equip most nonprofit executives to determine which research purposes and methodologies they should discuss with their development and research advisers. In addition, it should produce an understanding of basic research methodology that may prevent costly mistakes and misleading results from research that has employed inappropriate research techniques.

4

Designing the Questionnaire

In this chapter I provide an overview of the four basic principles, or goals, of questionnaire design: (1) screening to ensure the correct persons respond to the survey; (2) maximizing the response rate; (3) minimizing bias; and (4) constructing effective, actionable questions.

With a general understanding of these principles you will be better able to weave your specific questions into a questionnaire or interview, achieving more valid results. The chapter concludes with a discussion of the method and purpose of the questionnaire pretest.

Screening to Ensure the Correct Persons Respond

The first step in questionnaire design is to determine the degree to which the people in the sample correspond to the desired target population. If not every person who will receive the mailing or who will be called is a member of the desired population, screening questions will be necessary. Screening questions are designed to exclude inappropriate people from the survey. For example, if your nonprofit was conducting a fundraising event and you desired to conduct an on-site survey of all those attending, then there would likely be no reason for beginning each interview by asking screening questions. By definition, everyone you interview at that event qualifies just by being present. However, if it were desirable to administer the survey only to the current donors in attendance, some questions would need to be asked very early in the interview to exclude the people who were not donors.

In telephone surveys, screening questions are usually asked immediately following the introduction (discussed later in this chapter). This ensures that nonqualifying respondents are not inconvenienced any more than necessary, and it also makes better use of the survey interviewers' time. If a person does not qualify, the interviewer usually doesn't say, "You don't qualify." Instead, she simply thanks the person for his time.

Screening questions are commonly used to ensure that an appropriate member of each sample household is interviewed. The survey may seek a decision maker or someone with appropriate experience or awareness in some area. In this instance, if the person answering the phone does not qualify, he is asked whether someone else in the household matches the criteria sought.

Mail survey screening questions can be handled similarly, though it is important to be tactful. If a particular response disqualifies a person from the study and a notation to that effect is printed next to the response, some respondents may be tempted to alter their answers in order to qualify. One alternative is to direct nonqualifying respondents to *skip to* another question, bypassing a large portion of the questionnaire but completing a few demographic questions and then returning the survey. Such responses are not included in the survey results. This approach does not take too much of the respondent's time, and it preserves the integrity of the data.

When a nonprofit is recruiting for focus groups, screening questions also serve another purpose: they may ensure that the respondent is able to express himself or herself verbally. Because of the high cost per respondent in focus groups, it is especially important to ascertain in advance that each respondent is willing and able to participate actively and to follow instructions. A screening question with this purpose often asks prospective participants to describe something related to the subject being discussed. For example:

1. Please tell me about the mail you receive from charities.

Or the question could ask the prospective participant to respond with a list, in order to gauge her creativity and cooperation.

1. People give to charitable organizations for a number of reasons. Please list four possible reasons why a person would make a charitable donation.

In addition to screening respondents, the answers to these questions can provide useful insights even before the focus group convenes.

Maximizing the Response Rate

As discussed in Chapter Three, the response rate refers to the proportion of people who actually complete the questionnaire out of all those to whom the questionnaire has been offered. The higher the response rate, the more likely the results are to be valid, and vice versa. Getting the best response rate you can is absolutely critical if you are to obtain valid survey results. Nevertheless, this is possibly the most violated principle in market research today. Here are several important principles to keep in mind when designing a survey likely to maximize your response rate.

Get Off to a Good Start

The questionnaire introduction is the place to motivate the respondent to complete the questionnaire. An effective introduction will do the following:

- Identify the organization that initiated the survey. (As discussed later in this chapter, the organization may remain anonymous, to avoid creating bias. In this case the survey is called a *blind* survey.)
- State what the survey is about.

- Explain why the respondent should complete it, emphasizing any benefits.
- Encourage the respondent by pointing out that his or her opinions and experiences are important and that there are no right or wrong answers.
- Be concise, especially for phone surveys.

For mail surveys this introductory information appears in a cover letter. It is usually best if the cover letter is printed on the organization's letterhead and originates from a respected leader, such as the executive director, the chairperson of the board, or a sponsoring celebrity. It is also important to begin the questionnaire itself with a few introductory sentences so that the respondent will know how to complete and return the questionnaire even if the cover letter has become separated.

For both phone surveys and mail surveys it is also important to ask the respondent's permission. For example, at the end of the introduction to a phone survey, it is appropriate for the interviewer to say, "May I ask the first question?" To move directly from the introduction to the first question is presumptuous and disrespectful; it borders on being rude. When individuals say they do not have time to answer the survey, interviewers should try to schedule a time to call back. Telephone survey software, often called CATI (computer-assisted telephone interviewing) software, can manage this task. The interviewer inputs the callback time, and the software program generates the respondent's name at the correct time to the next available interviewer.

Some experts advocate telling the respondent up front approximately how long the survey takes to complete. If it is a short survey, this is a good idea, because the respondent is more likely to begin it knowing that it will not cost him or her much time. However, if the survey is longer than ten minutes, I suggest stating the expected duration only if requested. Routinely mentioning a time longer than ten minutes may cause an unacceptable proportion of respondents to decide they will not participate. In either event, it is important that the time quoted not be overly optimistic. For example, the interviewer should not say, "It will only be a few minutes," when the interview usually takes fifteen to twenty minutes. Besides being dishonest, this tactic reflects negatively on all survey researchers and damages the industry's credibility. Stating an estimated completion time for a mail survey is not necessary because the respondent can easily scan the survey and estimate the time based on his own abilities and experience.

Examples of introductions to a telephone and a mail survey, respectively, are displayed in Exhibits 4.1 and 4.2.

Consider Encouraging Respondents with an Incentive

Offering respondents money or another item of value is a standard method of maximizing response for commercial research projects. Such incentives may be conditional, available to respondents only

Exhibit 4.1 Sample Introduction to a Blind Telephone Survey.

Hello, I'm [name] with Campbell Research. We are conducting a national survey intended to help charities do a better job of serving the public, and would like to include your opinions and experiences. I will not ask for any money, and all your answers will remain confidential. May I ask the first question? [If "no" say, "You were selected to represent hundreds of others like yourself, and therefore your answers are very important. May we call you back at a more convenient time?"]

Exhibit 4.2 Sample Introduction to a Mail Survey.

The XYZ Nonprofit desires to produce publications that both inspire and inform our friends concerning our work. The purpose of this survey is to improve our publication *Charitable Times* by learning our friends' opinions about it and also what our friends need from it. Please take a few minutes to complete this survey and return it in the enclosed postage-paid envelope by March 31. Your participation and counsel in this survey are highly valued. Thank you for your assistance!

---

after they have completed the survey or focus group, or they may be unconditional, freely distributed in the mail in order to gain people's attention and encourage an informal sense of obligation to participate.

In the different environment of nonprofit research, incentives may be effective in some cases but very ineffective in others. Incentives may be ineffective with current donors, for example, because they are likely to view their participation as another way of contributing to the organization. Moreover, organizations that rely heavily on private donations will likely be chastised by donors for wasting funds with such tactics as enclosing dollar bills in a mail survey. However, constituents may be quite motivated by the information that a major donor has agreed to match every completed survey with a particular gift amount (the information must be true of course). Likewise, entering respondents' names in a prize drawing for a gift membership, a keepsake with the organization's logo, or some other item of value that relates to the organization or to its purpose can be appropriate.

These approaches may be used with any methodology. But there are some cautions. An incentive should be something that will be valued by everyone in the population being surveyed, otherwise it can lead to severe bias in the response. For example, a college alumni survey that offers to enroll participants in a prize drawing for basketball season tickets is likely to receive a disproportionately large number of responses from local alumni with a high interest in athletics. Also, prize drawings require respondents to reveal their identity, and they might then respond less openly and truthfully than they would to a survey on which they could remain anonymous. Finally, in some states, prize drawings are subject to fairly stringent disclosure laws.

Be Sensitive to the Respondent's Feelings

Being sensitive to the possibility that respondents may become discouraged or uncomfortable and fail to complete the survey requires the survey designer to use her own common sense. Simply put yourself in the respondents' shoes, and try to think how you would feel if you were answering the questionnaire. For example, if a lot of complex questions are asked at the beginning, people may decide the survey requires too much effort. Likewise, if unduly personal questions, such as those pertaining to age, income, or donation history, are asked too early, people may feel uncomfortable and quit. Reserve these difficult questions for later. When it is time to use them, consider interspersing them with less threatening, easy-to-answer questions, so the survey process does not get bogged down.

The first few questions should be easy to answer. Place the more difficult questions between the middle and the end of the interview. Often it is helpful to place the demographic questions about age, income, race, education, and so on, at the very end. Demographic questions do not usually produce the core of the content you are after, so if a person does not wish to answer them or quits for some other reason before reaching them, you will have lost less of the substantive data than you would have otherwise. One way to obtain answers to demographic questions that respondents are likely to perceive as highly personal is to ask them in a way that sounds routine. For example, in a telephone survey they could be introduced this way: "Thank you very much for your help! That completes the main portion of the survey. I now have only a few questions to ask for statistical classification purposes. What is your age?"

Use Logical Sequencing

Whether consciously or unconsciously, respondents are encouraged to remain in the process when they sense some logic to the order of the survey. Possibly this order reduces any confusion they might feel or maybe it makes it easier for them to step mentally from one subject to the next. When my colleagues and I construct a questionnaire for a typical donor survey, we generally start by asking respondents about their impressions of the nonprofit sector generally, and later we ask specific questions regarding the sponsoring nonprofit. When asking these specific questions, we tend to group them so we ask about the respondents' general perceptions, then about their communications preferences, and finally (because this topic is a little more sensitive), about what might motivate them to donate more or, conversely, what might cause them to discontinue their support. Questionnaires that inquire about events occurring over time might best be organized chronologically. For example, a donor survey might start by asking how respondents first heard of the organization, then what motivated them to give the first time, then what has kept them involved, and finally, what improvements they would like to see.

Pay Attention to Questionnaire Length

Probably everyone reading this book has terminated his or her response to a survey simply because it was taking too long. Simply looking at the number of pages and the size of the print of a mail survey might be intimidating enough to make a person to drop the survey into the "circular file." The ideal length for a mail survey is four standard pages. It can be printed on both sides of an 11-by-17-inch sheet of paper, which is then folded once to produce a booklet consisting of four 8½-by-11-inch pages. The nice thing about this format is that it is not stapled. Stapling can require respondents to flip or reverse pages, which is awkward and tedious and may easily cause them to miss pages or to toss the whole questionnaire. The maximum mail survey size should be no more than eight pages. I once heard of a large nonprofit that sent out thirteen-page questionnaires to its current donors. These donors gave an average of $250 per year and were very loyal, but even among this group the response rate was a low 30 percent, likely because of the lengthy questionnaire.

Telephone surveys are usually considered convenient when they take five to ten minutes to complete; up to twenty minutes is still reasonable, however. Expect poor results and irritated constituents if the survey takes twenty-five minutes or more.

In-person interviews are similar to telephone interviews, but the amount of time people will consider reasonable depends a great deal on the circumstances under which the interview is conducted. For example, if the survey is being administered at an event right before the main act, respondents are likely to be restless and distracted. The same goes for respondents who are asked for an interview when they are heading for home after an evening event.

Use Skipping as Needed

Have you ever taken a survey that asks a question that ignores information you just gave? For example, let's say you just answered a question about your marital status by saying, "Never married." Then the next question asks you how many years you have been married! It is frustrating for respondents when they are asked superfluous questions. They may feel that their time is being wasted and that the questionnaire was not thoughtfully designed. In any event the likelihood that they will not complete the survey is heightened. To maximize response, both mail and phone questionnaires should direct respondents past inappropriate questions, using the *skip to* phrase, as in this example:

1. Have you ever been married?
   1. Yes
   2. No (skip to Question 4)
2. Have you ever been divorced?

Minimizing Bias

What good is a survey if its very design skews the answers? The results can be worse than useless—they can be misleading. For this reason it is critical that the designer of the questionnaire take pains to be certain there is no inherent bias in the questions. Here are some steps to take to avoid creating bias in your questionnaire.

Avoid Unnecessary Words That May Stir Emotions

The language of the questionnaire may cause reactions that distort the information you are looking for. For example, the word *Democrat* in the following question about legislation could stir the feelings of a respondent either for or against the legislation, regardless of its actual content, depending on how the respondent feels about the Democratic Party:

1. Do you feel that the Democrat-initiated House bill HB-119 is good?

    1. Yes
    2. No

Ensure Descriptive Information Is Necessary and Objective

Sometimes background information is necessary. If so, ensure that it is objective. For example, this question could lead to biased answers:

1. Building a performing arts complex will cost $5 million and bring great pride to our city. Do you think the necessary bond issue will be worthwhile?

    1. Yes
    2. No

On the one hand, mentioning that the project will cost $5 million is necessary for the respondent to determine whether the project is worthwhile. On the other hand, the statement that the project will "bring great pride to our city" is an opinion, and therefore it should be omitted.

Avoid Dual-Issue Questions

Sometimes a researcher will construct a question that simultaneously asks about two items, assuming that the answer to both will be the same. As a result the respondent may not know how to answer the question. Moreover, the analyst will not be able to interpret the results of the answers the question does receive. Consider the following example:

1. Are you comfortable with the frequency and tone of the museum's appeals?

People may be comfortable with the tone but not the frequency, or vice versa. On the back end, will the researcher be able to affirm with certainty how the respondents feel about each item, tone on the one hand and frequency on the other? No. As a result the nonprofit will not know whether to try to improve the tone, the frequency, or both.

Offer All Reasonable Possible Responses

Respondents may quickly become frustrated if the answer that accurately reflects their opinion is not offered as a possibility. Consider this example:

1. In what geographical regions do you feel it is most important for the ABC Nonprofit to concentrate its efforts?
   1. Africa
   2. Latin America
   3. Eastern Europe and the Commonwealth of Independent States (CIS)
   4. United States
   5. Far East

Many regions, such as Australia, the Middle East, Canada, and the Indian subcontinent, are not offered among these possible answers. It would be better to form a more inclusive list or at least to offer *other* as an option.

Here is another example. See if you can tell which response is missing:

1. How successful do you feel the XYZ Nonprofit has been at fulfilling its goals?
   1. Very successful

2. Somewhat successful
3. Not too successful

The missing response is *don't know*. (In fact, almost 40 percent of the donors to major health charities give this answer.) If the respondent feels he cannot answer a question, the telephone interviewer needs to know what data to record. The don't know option should not be read by the interviewer but accepted and recorded if initiated by the respondent. If don't know is not available, the interviewer may select one of the available responses rather than have it look as though the question was skipped. Including a don't know option in a mail survey is not usually necessary; if the respondent doesn't like the choices given, she is likely to simply skip the question.

Constructing Effective, Actionable Questions

The first half of this chapter discussed three of the principles of questionnaire design: screening to ensure the correct persons respond to the survey, maximizing the response rate, and minimizing bias. To accomplish the fourth principle of constructing effective, actionable questions, we must understand the methodology for designing questions and answers, the building blocks of questionnaires.

A questionnaire designer can ask different types of questions designed to elicit different types of responses. The most basic categorization is that of *closed-ended* versus *open-ended* questions. As their name implies, closed-ended questions are those that offer a finite number of predetermined responses. All the example questions presented earlier in this chapter are closed-ended questions. Open-ended questions do not offer any prespecified answers; the respondent may answer however she likes. Here are two examples of open-ended questions:

1. How do you feel the ABC Nonprofit could improve its service to you as a donor?

2. What type of shows would you like the ABC Broadcasting Network to air?

In order to provide you with a better sense of when to use each type of question, here is a summary of their advantages and disadvantages.

Open-Ended Questions

The main disadvantage of open-ended questions is exemplified by a call I received one day from a nonprofit seeking help with a questionnaire that contained ten open-ended questions. The staff were wondering how they were going to summarize the results once the one thousand or so responses had been tallied! By not giving people a fixed set of choices, the questionnaire designer had left herself open to many hours of painstaking research on the back end.

A typical telephone survey may result in anywhere from four hundred to one thousand completed questionnaires with seventy responses per questionnaire. This implies a total of up to seventy thousand responses! If each response was to an open-ended question, it would be overwhelming to enter all these answers into a computer. In addition, before the organization could perform a quantitative analysis of these responses, categories would have to be created to classify the thoughts. Using closed-ended questions makes this stage a lot easier because each answer can be entered with a single key stroke and then statistically analyzed.

Another disadvantage of open-ended questions is that they require the respondents to think harder. As a result respondents are less likely to answer these questions. Also, when they do respond, they may not answer the actual question. For example, a common response to the question, "How can the XYZ Nonprofit improve?" is the nonanswer, "XYZ is doing a great job!" It is for these reasons that surveys typically include no more than one or two open-ended questions.

The advantage of open-ended questions is that the respondents are not constrained to the choices the researcher offers. This is especially helpful when the researcher does not have a very clear idea of the different types of responses the population might offer. When a survey seems to require a great many open-ended questions, it may be best to conduct qualitative research by such means as focus groups before fielding the survey. Then, based on the qualitative research results, closed-ended questions can be formulated.

Closed-Ended Questions

Four advantages of closed-ended questions are that the fixed answers (1) help respondents better understand the questions, (2) aid respondents in thinking of possible answers, (3) reduce irrelevant answers, and (4) produce answers that are more specific and easier to classify. Consider, for example, how varied the responses might be to this open-ended question:

1. How much education do you have?

Here is how this question would look as a closed-ended question:

1. What is the highest level of education you have completed?
    1. Some high school
    2. High school diploma
    3. Some college
    4. Four-year college degree
    5. Graduate degree

Alternative Types of Questions

Two additional question types offer some of the features of both open- and closed-ended questions.

Closed-Ended Questions with an Open Option. Sometimes the researcher will have a good idea of most of the possible answers but will still want to offer respondents an opportunity to provide their own answers. This is accomplished by offering *other* as one of the options.

1. What type of musicals would you like the Metropolitan Performing Arts Center to offer?

    1. Comedy

    2. Drama

    3. Horror

    4. Other (please specify): _____

Unprompted Questions. Sometimes the interviewee is asked a question that requires a simple answer, but he is not given any choices. This unprompted question format will work only for telephone and in-person surveys, not mail surveys. An example is this telephone survey question:

1. Some nonprofits invite donors to sponsor a child. For these sponsorships, the donor typically gives a specific amount every month—such as $20. The nonprofit uses this money to assist with a specific child's education, food, and medical expenses. What child sponsorship agencies are you familiar with, if any? [**Do not prompt.**]

    1. World Vision

    2. Save the Children

    3. Christian Children's Fund

    4. Compassion International

    5. Childreach

    6. Children International

    7. Other _____

    8. Don't know

Unprompted questions, that is questions that have a fixed list of answers that the interviewer does not read for the respondent, can provide some of the benefits of open-ended questions in that the response is reflective of each respondent's thinking, unbiased by the power of suggestion. Yet the telephone interviewer has a specific selection to mark and does not have to write out an answer that will have to be coded and categorized later. This question format is often used to ascertain a population's *unaided awareness* of the nonprofit and of competing organizations.

Types of Closed-Answer Formats

Answers to questions can be constructed many different ways. Here are a number of different fixed-answer formats to choose from.

Multiple Choice. Multiple choice is probably the most common response format. It is used when the data to be gathered are *categorical* (also referred to as *nominal*). Categorical data are nonnumeric, nonordinal data. The sample questions shown earlier on the topics of musicals and child sponsorship charities have categorical responses. The following is a third example:

1. What is your race?
    1. African American
    2. Asian
    3. Caucasian
    4. Hispanic
    5. Other

Rating Scale. A rating scale is a set of responses that implies a logical order, as in the following example:

1. How do you feel about the programming of your local public radio station? Would you say you are

Very Satisfied	Satisfied	Dissatisfied	Very Dissatisfied
1	2	3	4

Likert Scale. The Likert scale is a rating scale that usually has a total of five, seven, or nine responses ranging between two extremes (for example, strongly agree versus strongly disagree). The intensity of each response option is symmetrical, and the middle response option indicates neutrality. Converting the public radio question with the basic ordinal answer scale to a question with a Likert scale produces this question:

1. How do you feel about the programming on your local public radio station? Would you say you are

Very Satisfied	Satisfied	Neutral	Dissatisfied	Very Dissatisfied
1	2	3	4	5

Interval Scale. Some questions use an interval scale, which provides the most exact information. It is a mathematical scale in which each segment of the scale represents an exact measurement. Interval scales might address, for example, the actual value for a respondent's income, age, number of months since last gift, number of years as a donor or member, size of largest donation, and so forth. (*Ranges* of values, such as ages twenty-one to thirty, thirty-one to forty, and so forth, are ordinal, not interval, scales.) Rating scales of seven points or more are also considered valid interval scales, as in this example:

1. On a scale of 1 to 10, where 10 is *completely satisfied* and 1 is *completely dissatisfied*, please rate your overall satisfaction with our newsletter.

1	2	3	4	5	6	7	8	9	10

Order of Response Options

The order in which response options are offered is very important. For best results, the order should be logical so that the answers do not confuse the respondent. This logic will also help telephone respondents remember the answers they hear. For example, the answer scales for the sample questions about public radio programming have a logical order, whereas an arrangement such as the following for scale items is counterintuitive and might motivate the respondent to shut down the interview:

1. How do you feel about the programming on your local public radio station? Would you say you are

Dissatisfied	Neutral	Satisfied	Very Satisfied	Very Dissatisfied
1	2	3	4	5

Rotation of Questions and Responses

When scales such as the kinds just described are used in telephone surveys, the order of the answer items should be rotated if at all possible from interview to interview. The reason for this step is that some people have a tendency to choose the first response offered. Therefore, when a series of questions having possible responses ranging from very satisfied to very dissatisfied is asked during a phone or in-person survey, there might be a bias in a respondent's answers toward the very satisfied end of the spectrum. To compensate for this bias, the response order can be rotated so that half the participants hear the responses in the logical order from very satisfied to very dissatisfied and the other half hear the responses in the logical order from very dissatisfied to very satisfied.

Although it is advantageous to use answer rotation in a mail survey as well, it is often cost prohibitive. Nevertheless, when necessary, questions and response lists for a mail survey can be rotated by creating two (or more) versions of the questionnaire, and perhaps printing each version on a different color to distinguish them from one another. This approach, however, requires that all but one questionnaire version be derotated during data entry to produce a single, consistent data set. (That is, if 1 represents very satisfied on one set of questionnaires and 1 represents very dissatisfied on a second set, the answers on one of the sets will have to be reversed before the data can be entered consistently and produce valid results.) This additional step represents an additional opportunity for error—which could prove to be far more damaging than the potential bias that rotation seeks to guard against. Fortunately, rotation is less critical for a mail survey because respondents can scan up and down the possible responses quickly, allotting each possible answer equal attention and weight.

Categorical answers may be placed in alphabetical order (for example, African American, Asian, Caucasian, Hispanic), but this usually does not make a difference in a phone or in-person survey because the pertinent answer should be obvious to the respondent. For a mail survey it is a nice touch to alphabetize items but not at all critical. Ideally, however, all lists of fixed answers in telephone surveys, whether consisting of words or numbers, will be rotated, preferably using CATI software.

Questionnaire Approval and Pretest

Once the first draft of the questionnaire is complete, it should be submitted to the authorizing person or committee, as described in Chapter Two. The members of the authorizing body should be encouraged to suggest whatever improvements they can. It is my experience that the questionnaires that receive the most scrutiny by the largest number of appropriate people achieve the best results. This approval process also builds a sense of involvement and ownership among those who will be responsible for making decisions based on research information. Drafts should go back and forth until all suggestions are implemented as well as possible. When the final draft is in hand, it is time for the pretest. The authorizing person or committee should be aware that the pretest will almost certainly reveal the need for further changes. Typically, an agreement has been reached beforehand that if the changes are minor and nonsubstantive, they will simply be made and the survey will be implemented. If, however, any questions need to be omitted or changed substantially, the questionnaire will be sent back to the authorizing person or committee for a final approval.

The pretest is one of the most important parts of the questionnaire design process. A good pretest can catch a multitude of errors with the potential to lower response rate, create bias, and affect validity. As its name implies, the pretest is an experimental administration of the questionnaire to a small number of people before it is administered to the entire sample.

It is ideal if the pretest can be conducted with a small subset of the sample to be used, because this will ensure that the backgrounds, ages, and educational levels of those taking the pretest are roughly the same as the demographics of those in the ultimate audience. Sometimes, however, it is not practical to administer the questionnaire to a portion of the sample. In these cases, you may administer the pretest to a group that is reasonably similar. For example, if the survey is to be administered via mail to the volunteers in a national organization, conducting the pretest by mailing the questionnaire to a small sample of volunteers nationally would be ideal, but it may also be too time consuming. Instead, the questionnaire can be pretested with the volunteers present on a particular day at the local chapter of the organization. This can be effective because the purpose is not to obtain statistically reliable results. Rather it is to see how the questionnaire might be improved from the respondents' point of view. Improvements are often needed after the pretest to increase the likelihood of completion and therefore the response rate and to increase clarity and therefore validity. The pretest should answer such questions as these:

- Is the introduction sufficiently motivating?
- Do respondents clearly understand the questionnaire?
- Is any of the terminology too difficult?
- Does the questionnaire assume an inappropriately low level of respondent knowledge, so that it drags on too slowly for respondents?
- Is the questionnaire too wordy?
- Is there unnecessary redundancy?
- Do all the questions offer all possible response options?
- Are all response options mutually exclusive (to make it easier to select among them)?
- Are there places in the questionnaire that cause respondent

confusion or irritation, resulting in a tendency for the respondent to shut down the interview or stop marking answers on the form?

- Is the interview or written list of questions an appropriate length?

Additionally, the pretest should reveal whether the questions elicit responses that address the research objectives, providing the kind of information the organization is seeking.

There is also one particular advantage to administering the pretest for a mail survey to a local sample. It allows the researcher to be present so that she can discuss with the respondents the aspects of the questionnaire that seem confusing, unclear, too difficult, and the like. This may be done in a group setting or individually. The researcher may also wish to give those taking the pretest a brief questionnaire about the questionnaire, asking whether any aspects of the questionnaire seemed unclear or difficult to understand and whether they felt frustrated at any point.

Conducting the pretest for a telephone survey is easier, and this pretest may produce more information than a mail survey pretest. For the phone survey pretest, the researcher does not have to seek a similar sample but can use a portion of the actual survey sample. Either the researcher or an experienced and observant interviewer may conduct the pretest. He or she needs to be sensitive to any difficulties or confusion respondents may have, jotting down notes in the margin of the questionnaire about the parts that are flowing and those that are not, and why.

A pretest usually aims to collect twenty to fifty completed questionnaires. Once the results of the test have been examined, the questionnaire should be revised appropriately. As described earlier, if the changes are minor, the survey is fielded once they have been made. If substantive edits are needed, the questionnaire is sent to the authorizing person or committee for a final approval. Approval having been obtained, the questionnaire is ready to be administered.

Conclusion

In this chapter I have shared a variety of principles to follow when designing a questionnaire. The next chapter offers highly specific examples of ways to format questions effectively and details the nonprofit topics that might be addressed by the questionnaire.

5

Designing Individual Questions

In the fourth chapter I shared some of the general principles of questionnaire design. In this chapter I focus on the effective design of individual questions. In the next chapter I will illustrate putting all this information together to develop an actual questionnaire.

There are ten action steps in the development of an effective, actionable question.

Step 1. Determine the Key Word or Concept

The first challenge in writing a good question is determining what type of answer you are looking for. Then you must decide on the key word or concept you want to the respondent to focus on in his response. Do you want to learn how *important* some aspect of your non-profit's program is? Or maybe you are looking to determine how *aware* or *interested* or *satisfied* or *motivated to donate* a person is. Or maybe you are seeking to determine to what extent respondents *agree* with something. It is critical that you identify the key word that will guide people's input and give you the information you most want.

Step 2. Write a Rough Draft of the Question

Don't be worried about writing the perfect question right away, but do begin to write each question early on. Write it out as best you can, using the key word or concept you have identified and including the possible answers if it is likely to be a closed-ended question, with the understanding that you will refine it in the remaining action steps. The act of writing out questions and possible responses will sharpen your focus on the information you want, and it will stimulate your thinking about how to draw that information out of the respondents.

Step 3. Determine What Information the Respondent Needs

Generally, a question should supply information about the question topic only if necessary. First, providing preliminary information may introduce a bias, which will defeat your purpose. Second, it is not realistic. After all, you are sampling a population to learn how the average person feels about a topic, but if you share information, especially new information, about that topic, you may have just given your sample knowledge that your general population is not privy to, and therefore the results you obtain will not reflect the current views of that population. Even so, there are times when giving preliminary information is necessary, so ask yourself whether the respondent needs any information she does not already have in order to answer the question.

For example, a nonprofit that needs to make some decisions about promoting a particular program may want to learn both the respondents' current awareness of the program and their interest in the program. Learning the level of interest may require describing the program briefly to respondents who say they are not aware of it.

Step 4. Review the Question with Respect to the Four Design Principles and Improve It as Indicated

Examine each question in the light of the four design principles discussed in Chapter Four: (1) screening to ensure the correct persons respond to the survey; (2) maximizing the response rate; (3) minimizing bias; and (4) constructing effective, actionable questions. Often, nonprofit executives assume their constituents have far more awareness and knowledge of the organization than they do. Therefore it is always good to ask yourself, Are the people we are interviewing capable of providing the information we are requesting of them? If not, you should consider whether it would be better to ask the same question of different people or to ask a different question of the people in the existing sample.

Will the question be perceived negatively by some respondents, tempting them to drop out early and affecting the response rate? Of course people may react negatively to a question perceived as too personal, but there are other pitfalls to avoid. These include questions that have obvious answers or that imply certain responses are more acceptable than others and questions that are hard to understand or that pose an unreasonable number of choices to remember. Will the wording of the question lead to biased responses—either to that question or to other questions?

Finally, will the responses provide information that is insightful and actionable? Sometimes it is good to ask yourself, What things might we change or do differently based on the results of this question? If your answer is "nothing," reexamine the reason for asking the question.

Step 5. Determine Whether Similar Questions Should Be Designed as a Battery of Questions

Sometimes the same type of information is needed for each of a number of aspects of a larger topic. In these cases it is more efficient for you and respondent if you ask the general question just once and follow it with a series of subquestions with the same set of response options for each one. Here are two examples of batteries of questions as they might be used in a telephone survey. Note that the *don't know* option is available for the interviewer to mark but is not offered directly to the respondent.

1. Please indicate whether you agree completely, somewhat, a little, or not at all that each of the following statements is true of the ABC Drug Rehabilitation Program.

	Completely Agree	Somewhat Agree	Agree a Little	Don't Agree	Don't Know
1. It is in need of donations.	1	2	3	4	5
2. It successfully changes lives.	1	2	3	4	5
3. It is successful in helping people avoid becoming drug addicts and alcoholics.	1	2	3	4	5
4. It is successful in rehabilitating drug addicts and alcoholics.	1	2	3	4	5
5. It demonstrates financial integrity.	1	2	3	4	5
6. It uses donations well; they have a strong beneficial impact.	1	2	3	4	5
7. It does an excellent job of communicating its accomplishments and results.	1	2	3	4	5

2. How helpful do you find the following aspects of the XYZ Nonprofit newsletter? Do you usually find the [read aspect] *very helpful, somewhat helpful, not too helpful, or not at all helpful?*

	Very Helpful	Somewhat Helpful	Not Too Helpful	Not at All Helpful	Don't Know
1. Feature articles	1	2	3	4	5
2. Editorial from the director	1	2	3	4	5
3. Pass-It-On section	1	2	3	4	5
4. Resources page (books and pamphlets for sale)	1	2	3	4	5
5. Letters from readers	1	2	3	4	5

Batteries of questions, as long as they do not contain more than about twelve items, are good to ask because they produce a lot of information and yet are relatively easy to answer. The respondent can answer many subquestions quickly and easily because he does not have to adjust to a new frame of questioning and a new set of response options with each item. The information from question batteries also produces consistently formatted data, allowing useful comparisons among the battery items.

Step 6. Determine Whether the Question Can Have a Simple Set of Response Options

Each of your questions can be answered with varying degrees of specificity. You need to determine how precise the answer to each question needs to be. Depending on the information your nonprofit needs, you may be able to make the response options for some questions very simple, with no gradation. For example, a question might ask respondents whether they *generally like* or *generally do not like* something. Similarly, it might ask them to answer *true* or *false*, *yes* or *no*, and so forth. These response sets that offer only two choices are the easiest for people to answer. A respondent is more likely to continue answering a questionnaire with these easy answers than to complete a questionnaire that requires more precise and therefore more difficult to determine answers. Thus simple response choices will increase response rate and survey accuracy. If simple, two-choice answers will give you the information you are looking for, use them.

Step 7. If the Question Requires More Than Two Response Options, Determine Whether They Are Categorical or Represent a Continuum

Sometimes your research purposes will require a finer gradation in an answer than two choices will afford. Many issues cannot be reduced to yes or no or like or dislike judgments. Sometimes the nonprofit needs to know the degree of donor approval or agreement in order to make a sound decision. This is especially true for surveys that are repeated at given intervals in order to track changes in attitudes over time.

For each question that needs more than the simplest response option, you need to determine whether the possible response options should represent categories or a continuum. Categories, as discussed in Chapter Four, are nonnumeric and nonordinal. They might be, for example, the ways people first learned about the organization or demographic characteristics. Here is an example:

1. What national health organizations are you familiar with, if any?

    1. American Heart Association
    2. American Cancer Society
    3. American Lung Association
    4. Alzheimer's Association
    5. National Multiple Sclerosis Society
    6. March of Dimes
    7. Other _____

The continuum answer option offers varying levels of agreement or disagreement, as shown in the examples for Step 5.

Step 8. If the Response Options Reflect a Continuum, Determine the Continuum Type

There are at least three types of continua: unidirectional, bidirectional, and 0 percent to 100 percent. Bidirectional continua are probably the most readily understood. They range from one extreme to the opposite extreme. For example, a continuum might range from *agree very strongly* to *disagree very strongly*, or from *I want to receive many more communications of this type* to *I want to receive many less communications of this type*. When using a bidirectional response continuum, you need to decide whether it should offer a neutral, midpoint option, such as *neither satisfied or dissatisfied*. This option is recommended unless a neutral answer will not be helpful for the nonprofit's purposes (it may need to make a change one way or the other to the status quo, for example) and you suspect that many respondents will select it. By dropping the neutral option, you can encourage respondents to give an opinion one way or the other. This may frustrate respondents, however, and therefore should not be done often.

The next thing to decide is how many gradations of response you will offer for each end of the spectrum. It is best to offer the lowest number that will still achieve your information objective because this makes answering easier for the respondent. Generally, allowing one or two options at each end is best. Here is one example of response options with bidirectional continua. It is a battery of questions, with one response option on each extreme and one neutral option:

1. Charities use a number of methods to communicate with donors through the mail. I will name some. With regard to [read method] do you feel the ABC Health Charity does this *too often, not often enough,* or *about the right amount?*

	Too Often	About the Right Amount	Not Often Enough	Don't Know
1. Including the personal stories of disabled people	1	2	3	4
2. Including photos of disabled people	1	2	3	4
3. Enclosing sweepstakes tickets with a letter asking for a donation	1	2	3	4
4. Enclosing a free gift with a letter asking for a donation	1	2	3	4
5. Enclosing name and address labels with a letter asking for a donation	1	2	3	4
6. Enclosing a calendar with a letter asking for a donation	1	2	3	4

7. Sending standard appeal letters that do not include a premium of any kind, such as seals or a calendar	1	2	3	4
8. Sharing details about what the ABC Health Charity is all about	1	2	3	4
9. Sharing details about what the ABC Health Charity has accomplished, such as the number of people it has helped, the number of programs it has, and similar accomplishments	1	2	3	4
10. Sharing financial information, such as how much money goes to overhead and how much to fight disease	1	2	3	4
11. Sending reminder appeals soon after a major appeal	1	2	3	4

Sometimes the question you need to have answered lends itself to a continuum response design, but you expect that most of the responses will be toward one end of the scale. In this case it will be more convenient for both you and the respondent if the answer options contain only the portion of the scale that is relevant, omitting the most extreme possible answer(s) on one or both ends of the scale. Unidirectional continua are often appropriate for nonprofit surveys, because they frequently ask members or donors about which organization services or program aspects they like best, and it is very rare for a donor or member to be vehemently opposed to a service of his or her own nonprofit; usually people simply prefer some aspects more than others. Here are two examples of questions with unidirectional response options:

1. How well informed do you feel you are regarding the XYZ Nonprofit's activities and accomplishments?

   1. Very informed
   2. Somewhat informed
   3. Not too informed
   4. Not at all informed
   5. Don't know

2. The ABC Health Charity offers a variety of inspirational resources. Please tell us how interested you are in each of the following resources. ["First"/"Next"] one is [read resource item]. Are you *very, somewhat,* or *not too interested* in these resources?

	Very Interested	Somewhat Interested	Not Too Interested	Don't Know
1. Books, pamphlets, and videos	1	2	3	4
2. Adult education curricula	1	2	3	4
3. Conferences and seminars	1	2	3	4
4. Children's education curricula	1	2	3	4
5. Audiocassettes	1	2	3	4

Finally, here is an example of a question that expects a response between 0 percent and 100 percent.

1. Of all those served by inner-city rescue missions, what percentage would you say are women and children ____%

Step 9. Put It All Together and Place the Question in the Questionnaire

Having read the principles in Chapter Four and having made the decisions called for in the previous steps in this chapter, take your best shot at writing the question and, if it is a closed-ended question, the fixed responses. (The sample questionnaires in Chapter Six provide more examples of questions and answers.) Then insert the question in the most appropriate place in the questionnaire.

Step 10. Pretest the Questionnaire and Refine It Accordingly

Rely on the pretest to help you improve your questions. As discussed in Chapter Four, the pretest involves administering your questionnaire to a small portion of the sample or to a similar group to obtain a preliminary indication of how well respondents understand the questions and are able to give appropriate answers. This will tell you which aspects of the questionnaire are working and which need improvement. Refine the questionnaire based on the pretest results.

Conclusion

This chapter has suggested a method for thinking through your questions from rough draft to final draft in order to develop a questionnaire with research quality questions. The next chapter shares two sample questionnaires to further illustrate how to design a questionnaire.

6

Putting It All Together

Chapter Four discussed basic principles of questionnaire design, and Chapter Five outlined a step-by-step method of designing individual questions. In this chapter I demonstrate by example how researchers weave these principles and action steps together to craft a questionnaire. I also introduce some additional questionnaire design principles.

A Telephone Questionnaire for Constituents

First, let's look at and discuss the sample questionnaire in Exhibit 6.1. It illustrates a telephone survey designed to solicit information from a nonprofit health agency's members and donors. It starts out as a blind survey; the respondents are not told the name of the sponsoring charity at first, only the name of the group conducting the research.

Contact Information
To begin with, because this is a telephone survey, the first item on the questionnaire is a short form for the interviewer to fill out. Sometimes the person who oversees the interviewers may need to identify the interviewer who completed a particular questionnaire. For this reason there are blanks for both the interviewer's and the respondent's names.

EXHIBIT 6.1 ABC Health Charity Telephone Questionnaire for Constituents.

Interviewer: _____ Rotation: <u>Yes</u> Date: _____ Survey No.: _____

Time Began: _____ Time Ended: _____ Zip Code: _____

Constituent Type: [Circle one:] Member Sustaining Member Donor Research Associate

Respondent Name: _____

Hello, I'm [give name] with Campbell Research. May I please speak with [respondent name]? We are conducting a national survey intended to help nonprofit health agencies and would like to include your opinions and experiences. I will not ask for any donations, and your answers will remain confidential. May I ask the first question? [If "no," say: "Your opinions are important to us. What time might be more convenient for us to call back?"]

1. Other than religious charities, what would you say are your three favorite charities? [If the respondent struggles with *favorite*, then ask which three come to his or her mind first. Record 1 for 1st, 2 for 2nd, and 3 for 3rd.]

American Red Cross	____	Disabled American Veterans	____
American Cancer Society	____	March of Dimes	____
American Heart Association	____	National Easter Seal Society	____
American Lung Association	____	National Wildlife Federation	____
ABC Health Charity	____	Paralyzed Veterans of America	____
United Cerebral Palsy Association	____	Salvation Army	____
Diabetes Foundation	____	Sierra Club	____
		Other:	____

2. I am going to read a list of statements that might be used to describe a health-related charity. For each statement, please tell me how important or unimportant it would be in your decision to make a donation to the charity. Using a 5-point scale on which 1 means *not at all important* and 5 means *extremely important*, how important would it be in your decision that the charity... **[read first/next]**?

	Not at All Important				Extremely Important
1. Is dedicated to helping children	1	2	3	4	5
2. Conducts research that will help those currently disabled and reduce the likelihood of others becoming disabled	1	2	3	4	5
3. Would use donations to help people in your area	1	2	3	4	5
4. Has helped to discover new medicines and techniques to alleviate people's suffering	1	2	3	4	5
5. Helps the disabled become independent	1	2	3	4	5
6. Is a reputable organization	1	2	3	4	5
7. Has already helped or could help someone you know	1	2	3	4	5
8. Maintains reasonable administrative and fundraising expenses	1	2	3	4	5
9. Supplies special medical equipment such as walkers and wheelchairs	1	2	3	4	5
10. Fights against a life-threatening disease like cancer or heart disease	1	2	3	4	5
11. Fights against a painful but non-life-threatening disease like arthritis	1	2	3	4	5

EXHIBIT 6.1 ABC Health Charity Telephone Questionnaire for Constituents, Cont'd.

3. In recent years people have become concerned about the way charities spend their donations. From the following list, choose the type of information that would help you be *most* confident that donated funds are well spent.

   1. The charity provides financial statements upon request.
   2. The charity publishes how much money goes toward its mission and how much toward overhead.
   3. The charity has been endorsed by a respected third party **[read only if asked: "For example, a national news magazine or a celebrity"].**
   4. The charity has been audited and approved by a national accounting firm.

4. I will read a list of things a health-related charity can do to improve its communication with its supporters. For each item, please share whether this action might be *very helpful* to you, be *somewhat helpful*, or *make no difference*. The **["first"/"next"]** action is that the charity . . . **[read first/next]**

	Very Helpful	Somewhat Helpful	Makes No Difference
1. Is featured on the news more for its work	1	2	3
2. Offers an 800 number through which you can listen to tapes regarding a disease and how to cope with it, and obtain research updates	1	2	3
3. Allows donors to send ideas to the charity's leadership and receive a personal response	1	2	3
4. Sends a thank-you note for each gift	1	2	3
5. Offers you membership that includes a newsletter or magazine	1	2	3

5. Today we are asking about a specific charity [pause], the ABC Health Charity. How well informed do you feel you are about the ABC Health Charity's activities and accomplishments?

   1. Very well informed
   2. Somewhat well informed
   3. Not too well informed
   4. Not at all informed
   5. Don't know [Don't prompt.]

6. How efficiently do you feel the ABC Health Charity uses the donations it receives? [If respondent chooses to circle 3 or 4, ask him or her to please explain.]

   1. Very efficiently
   2. Somewhat efficiently
   3. Not too efficiently; why? _____
   4. Not at all efficiently; why?
   5. Don't know [Don't prompt.]

7. Now I'm going to read a list of phrases that could be used to describe the ABC Health Charity. Please tell me how much you agree or disagree that each of the statements describes the ABC Health Charity. Using a 5-point scale, on which 5 means that you *agree completely* and 1 means that you *disagree completely*, to what extent do you agree that the ABC Health Charity . . . [read first/next]?

	Disagree Completely	Agree		Agree Completely	Don't Know
1. Is dedicated to helping children	1	2	3	4	5	6
2. Conducts research that will help those currently disabled and reduce the likelihood of others becoming disabled						
3. Would use donations to help people in your area	1	2	3	4	5	6

EXHIBIT 6.1 ABC Health Charity Telephone Questionnaire for Constituents, Cont'd.

4. Has helped to discover new medicines and techniques to alleviate people's suffering	1	2	3	4	5	6
5. Helps the disabled become independent	1	2	3	4	5	6
6. Is a reputable organization	1	2	3	4	5	6
7. Has already helped or could help someone you know	1	2	3	4	5	6
8. Maintains reasonable administrative and fundraising expenses	1	2	3	4	5	6
9. Supplies special medical equipment such as walkers and wheelchairs	1	2	3	4	5	6

8. The ABC Health Charity publishes a full-color, national magazine, called ABC *Health Today.* Are you familiar with it?

1. Yes   2. No   3. Don't know [**Don't prompt.**]

9. Some national health charities offer membership. Does the ABC Health Charity invite people to become members?

1. Yes   2. No   3. Don't know [**Don't prompt.**]

10. To the best of your knowledge, how are you involved with the ABC Health Charity, if at all? Are you a

1. Member
2. Sustaining Member
3. Regular donor
4. Research Associate
5. None of the above/not involved

11. **[Members and Sustaining Members only:]** There are a number of reasons why someone might choose to become a member. Please share whether the following aspects are *very*, *somewhat*, or *not too motivating* for you personally to become a member. The **["first"/"next"]** aspect is **[read first/next]**

	Very Motivating	Somewhat Motivating	Not Too Motivating
1. Receiving the *ABC Health Today* magazine	1	2	3
2. Because you have a chronic disease	1	2	3
3. Because someone you love has a chronic disease	1	2	3
4. To reduce the likelihood you or someone you love will suffer with a chronic disease someday	1	2	3

12. **[Members and Sustaining Members only:]** If you had a choice to receive the magazine or to have the cost of the magazine be applied to research or other services, which would you prefer?

1. Keep receiving the magazine
2. Rather have the money applied to research or other services

13. Charities use a number of methods to communicate with donors through the mail. I will ask whether you feel the ABC Health Charity uses these *too often* or *not often enough* or *about the right amount*. The **["first"/"next"]** one is **[read first/next]**

	Too Often	About the Right Amount	Not Often Enough	Don't Know [*Don't prompt.*]
1. Including *personal* stories about people with a chronic disease in its letters	1	2	3	4
2. Including photos of people with a chronic disease in its letters	1	2	3	4

EXHIBIT 6.1 ABC Health Charity Telephone Questionnaire for Constituents, Cont'd.

3. Sharing specifics about the purpose and goals of the ABC Health Charity	1	2	3	4
4. Sharing specifics about what the ABC Health Charity has accomplished (for example, the number of people helped, the number of programs it has, and so forth)	1	2	3	4
5. Sharing financial information (for example, how much money goes to fight disease and how much to overhead)	1	2	3	4
6. Sending thank-you letters and receipts, after receiving a donation	1	2	3	4

14. How do you feel about the quantity of mail you get from the ABC Health Charity? Compared with other charities, does the ABC Health Charity send

    1. More mail than average
    2. About average
    3. Less mail than average
    4. Don't know [**Don't prompt.**]

15. The ABC Health Charity communicates with its donors to inform them about its progress and to request donations. In addition to newsletters, it does this through mailings asking for financial support. How often do you remember receiving these mailings from the ABC Health Charity? Would you say

    1. More often than you would like
    2. About as often as you would like

3. Less often than you would like

4. **[Don't read:]** Don't receive them **[Skip to Question 18.]**

5. Don't know **[Don't prompt.]**

16. The following phrases could be used to describe the ABC Health Charity's letters asking for donations. Would you say these appeals are *very, somewhat, not too,* or *not at all* **[read first/next]**

	Very	Somewhat	Not Too	Not At All
1. Easy to understand	1	2	3	4
2. Oriented toward donations	1	2	3	4
3. Informative	1	2	3	4
4. Repetitive	1	2	3	4
5. Interesting	1	2	3	4
6. Guilt producing	1	2	3	4

17. What information would most motivate you to donate to the ABC Health Charity?

1. How many people it helps each year.

2. What services it performs

3. Success stories of individuals it has helped.

4. Educational information regarding its mission.

5. Financial information on how donations are spent.

EXHIBIT 6.1 ABC Health Charity Telephone Questionnaire for Constituents, Cont'd.

18. Charitable organizations may have a variety of people writing the letters requesting donations. Which person writing on behalf of the ABC Health Charity do you feel would *most* motivate you to donate?

   1.   The national chairperson of the ABC Health Charity

   2.   The chairperson of your local ABC Health Charity office?

   3.   A typical ABC Health Charity volunteer?

   4.   Don't know [**Don't prompt.**]

19. [**Donors and Research Associates only:**] I will read a list of reasons why people might donate to the ABC Health Charity. Please share whether you would be *very motivated, somewhat motivated,* or *not too motivated* to donate to the ABC Health Charity for that reason. The [**"first"/"next"**] reason is [**read first/next**].

	Very Motivating	Somewhat Motivating	Not Too Motivating
1. You have a chronic disease	1	2	3
2. Someone you love has a chronic disease	1	2	3
3. To reduce the likelihood that you or someone you love will suffer with a chronic disease someday	1	2	3
4. You receive from the ABC Health Charity information that helps you cope with a disease	1	2	3

20. What suggestions do you have about ways how the ABC Health Charity can improve either its work or its communications with you? _____

_____

_____

Thank you. This completes the main part of the survey. Now I just have some brief questions for confidential classification purposes.

21. What is your age?

    1. Under 25
    2. 25–30 years
    3. 31–35 years
    4. 36–40 years
    5. 41–45 years
    6. 46–50 years
    7. 51–55 years

    8. 56–60 years
    9. 61–70 years
    10. 71–75 years
    11. 76–80 years
    12. 81–85 years
    13. 86+ years

22. What is the highest level of education that you've completed?

    1. Some high school or less
    2. High school degree
    3. Vocational school
    4. Some college
    5. College degree
    6. Graduate degree

23. What is your race?

    1. Hispanic
    2. Caucasian
    3. African American

4. Asian
5. Native American
6. Other: _____

24. What is your marital status? Are you

1. Married
2. Single
3. Divorced or separated
4. Widowed

25. What would you say is your approximate annual household income?

1. Under $20,000	6. $60,001–$70,000
2. $20,001–$30,000	7. $70,001–$80,000
3. $30,001–$40,000	8. $80,000–$100,000
4. $40,001–$50,000	9. Over $100,000
5. $50,001–$60,000	10. Refused or don't know [**Don't prompt.**]

This concludes our survey. Thank you very much for your time and help. Have a great day! [**Terminate call.**]

26. Largest gift amount _____
27. Month and year of last gift _____
28. Year of first gift _____

The zip code is requested because for national surveys it is best to arrange the list of respondent names by time zone. Because this information is often not available on the original lists used to compile the interviewers' list, arranging that list by zip codes will approximate time zone information. If the list is sorted in zip code order, the zip code can also be used to find a respondent on the list if necessary. The "time began" and "time ended" blanks are especially useful during the pretest to learn the average time it takes to complete an interview. Sometimes a questionnaire is designed to accommodate several different subgroups, in this example the subgroups are the constituent types. It is best for the interviewer to clearly identify which group the respondent belongs to in the contact information on the front of the questionnaire, thus simplifying the later task of checking whether the desired quota for each subgroup has been met.

The Introduction

Every word of the introduction is critical. You should try to fulfill all the objectives of the introduction with as few words as possible. Note that it is important in a phone interview to assure the respondent that the interviewer will not be asking for any money. Also, to increase response rate and therefore accuracy, the interviewers encourage respondents who do not agree to take the survey to give a time when an interviewer can call back. The introduction also assures the respondent of confidentiality, and the interviewer asks each respondent's permission before beginning the questions.

Interviewer Instructions

The last part of the introduction is an instruction, or prompt, to the telephone interviewer. It is important to make it easy for the interviewer to distinguish between the words that are directed to her and those that she is to read to the respondent. Therefore instructions to the interviewer should be bracketed and printed in boldfaced type or with some other type of emphasis.

Initial Questions

The initial questions should be particularly easy to answer and not intrusive. People like to give their opinions. They want to feel important and that their opinion counts. Asking questions along these lines is especially encouraging to a respondent. Questions 1, 2, 3, and 4 all fall in this category.

The choice of initial questions in this survey is also directed by the fact that the survey starts out blind. Blind surveys (either partly or entirely blind) often represent better research, because the respondent is more likely to answer objectively. For example, if a donor understood right away that this survey was being conducted for a health charity he supports, he might provide more favorable answers, that is, ones he perceived as more acceptable, than he would if the survey were introduced as being about health organizations generally. So the initial four items focus on questions about health organizations in general. It is not until Question 5 that the first question is asked about a specific organization. By the end of a blind questionnaire people have often figured out who the survey sponsor is, but in the meantime, valuable, objective answers can be obtained. This approach may bother some respondents, however, who may view it as surreptitious, so it is best for small nonprofits with a tightly knit donor base not to use it. I also do not recommend using it with your major donors.

Note that it is much more difficult to conduct blind surveys by mail. First, the cover letter has to be from an objective third party retained to do the research, and this leads to a lower response rate than the charity could obtain by identifying itself. Second, all questions must be asked about several organizations or about organizations generally. And third, because the reply envelope must not specify the sponsoring organization by name, it too must go through the third party and is likely to be subject to a higher rate of postage than the nonprofit would normally pay.

General Evaluation Questions

Notice that general evaluation questions—such as, "How well informed do you feel about the ABC Health Charity's activities and accomplishments?" (Question 5), and, "How efficiently do you feel the ABC Health Charity uses the donations it receives?" (Question 6)—are asked early on. The questionnaire does not ask for a lot of information about specific respondent knowledge and opinions before asking these broad questions because the purpose of these general questions is to collect responses representative of the population from which the interviewees have been drawn. After the respondent has been asked to focus on what she knows or thinks, her answers to these broad questions might be more idiosyncratic and less representative.

Questions for Subgroups

This questionnaire contains some questions intended only for certain groups, Members and Sustaining Members on the one hand and Donors and Research Associates (the name given to the higher-level donors by the organization) on the other. The interviewer has the information about each respondent's status in the contact information and simply skips questions for which a particular respondent does not qualify.

Logical Flow

The questionnaire has a clear logical flow. After the initial blind questions come the general evaluative questions about the organization. Next come questions about membership (Questions 9 through 11) and then questions about communications (Questions 12 through 16), followed by questions about what motivates people to give to the charity (Questions 17 through 19). These questions about giving motivations are potentially personal and intrusive. They are placed toward the end of the questionnaire for two reasons. First, in the (fairly rare) event that a respondent is offended or just prefers not to answer, you will already have obtained most of the information your organization wanted. More important, placing these personal questions toward the end gives the interviewer time to establish some rapport and the respondent time to gain some momentum so that she is less likely to balk at answering.

The final question in the main section of the survey is an open-ended one, asking what suggestions the respondent might have to help the charity improve its work. This serves as a catch-all question, allowing the respondent to communicate anything she did not have an chance to share earlier.

The final section collects demographic information. These questions are placed at the end because they are the least critical to achieving the survey objectives, and they are not about the organization specifically. If someone quits prior to this point, the answers you have obtained will have been about more important issues than demographics. Another reason for placing these questions here is, again, that people may find them intrusive, especially the ones about age, income and education. Even when obtaining demographic information is a prime objective, do not begin with these questions. Place them in the middle or at the end, because they are so personal.

Types of Response Options

This questionnaire illustrates a variety of response options. For example, Question 1 asks for categorical responses, even though in this case the respondent must provide them himself.

Questions 2, 4, 7, 11, 13, 16, and 19 are batteries. Some people might see questions like Question 3 as battery questions at first glance, but note that this type has only one question and requires only one answer from the list of categorical answers given. Questions 8, 9, and 12 offer a simple response set, with just two choices. Question 11 is a unidirectional, ordinal response set, and Question 13 offers an example of a Likert Scale, being bidirectional and having a neutral option.

Further Respondent Information

At the very end of the questionnaire, there are a few more items for the interviewer to fill out. He transfers the information about previous contributions from the constituent database list to the questionnaire so that these key pieces of information and the constituent type can be entered into the computer along with all the survey results. These data can be used in a cross-tabulation analysis of the survey results, examining answers to a particular question according to categories from another question and noting statistically significant differences. For example, responses to Question 26 can be used to determine (for any question in the survey) how the larger donors' answers differed from those of the smaller donors. Similarly, responses to Question 27 can be used to determine how the results of recent givers differed from those of less recent givers, and responses to Question 27 can be used to show how donors' length of time on file correlates with survey answers.

A Mail Questionnaire for Members

Exhibit 6.2 is a mail questionnaire designed for an organization I will call the Beautiful Botanic Garden. It illustrates how an effective mail questionnaire might be laid out, and it offers ideas about successful questionnaire design for membership organizations, such as zoos, aquariums, museums, and botanic gardens.

The question and answer types described for the sample telephone survey can also be seen in this questionnaire. Therefore the following discussion focuses on those features important to mail questionnaires generally and also to membership surveys.

Graphic Design

Because the respondent will see the mail questionnaire, a lot more effort is put into it than into the typical phone questionnaire to make it attractive. Visual stimulation increases the likelihood that the respondent will spend enough time with the survey to complete it. At the same time it should be easy to use. The appearance of the questionnaire is discussed further in Chapter Seven.

EXHIBIT 6.2 Beautiful Botanic Garden Mail Questionnaire for Members.

Because you are a valued supporter of Beautiful Botanic Garden, your opinions are very important to us. To help us better meet your needs, please fill out this survey and return it in the enclosed postage-paid envelope by November 25, 2000, to Beautiful Botanic Garden, 1000 Washington Avenue, Some City, NY, 12345.

1. **How long have you been a member?**

   1 ☐ Less than a year
   2 ☐ 1 year
   3 ☐ 2–4 years
   4 ☐ 5 or more years
   5 ☐ I don't remember
   6 ☐ I'm no longer a member

2. **What is your current membership? If you are no longer a member what type of membership did you last have?**

   1 ☐ $25 Individual
   2 ☐ $35 Subscriber
   3 ☐ $50 Family/Dual
   4 ☐ $125 Special
   5 ☐ $300 Sponsor
   6 ☐ $500 Patron
   7 ☐ $1,200 Associate
   8 ☐ I don't remember

3. **How did you join Beautiful Botanic Garden?**

   1 ☐ Through the mail
   2 ☐ At the Garden
   3 ☐ Received as a gift
   4 ☐ Don't remember
   5 ☐ Other (*please specify*): _____

Note: This exhibit is an adaptation of a questionnaire that was printed on the four sides of a folded 11-by-17-inch sheet of paper.

4. Which membership benefits are most important to you?
(Please check one box for each benefit)

	Very Important (1)	Somewhat Important (2)	Not Too Important (3)	Don't Receive (4)
• Free admission to the Garden	☐	☐	☐	☐
• Reciprocal privileges at gardens across the country	☐	☐	☐	☐
• *Garden Gazette*	☐	☐	☐	☐
• Extended summer hours	☐	☐	☐	☐
• Summer Sunset Picnics	☐	☐	☐	☐
• Blossom Night/Members' Day	☐	☐	☐	☐
• Member-only Preview Nights	☐	☐	☐	☐
• Discounts on classes, family programs, trips, workshops	☐	☐	☐	☐
• Discount at Garden gift shop	☐	☐	☐	☐
• *Great Gardening Series* handbooks	☐	☐	☐	☐
• Discount at Colorful Cafe	☐	☐	☐	☐
• Parking passes	☐	☐	☐	☐
• *Custom plant(s)*	☐	☐	☐	☐

Comments: _____

5. **At higher levels of support you receive additional benefits. Which benefits would you be willing to pay more to receive?**

   (Please check one box for each benefit)

	Yes	No	No Opinion
• Parking passes	1 ☐	2 ☐	3 ☐
• *Custom plant(s)*	1 ☐	2 ☐	3 ☐
• Annual gift calendar	1 ☐	2 ☐	3 ☐
• *Great Gardening Series* handbooks	1 ☐	2 ☐	3 ☐
• *Garden Gazette*	1 ☐	2 ☐	3 ☐

6. **Which of the Garden's publications do you enjoy the most?**

   (Please check one box for each publication)

	Read Cover to Cover	Read Some Articles	Sometimes Scan	Don't Read at All
• *Member News*	1 ☐	2 ☐	3 ☐	4 ☐
• *Calendar of Events*	1 ☐	2 ☐	3 ☐	4 ☐
(The following are available to Subscriber or higher level members.)				
• *Garden Gazette*	1 ☐	2 ☐	3 ☐	4 ☐
• *Great Gardening Series* handbooks	1 ☐	2 ☐	3 ☐	4 ☐

7. How do you usually use your Garden publications?
(Please check one box for each publication)

	Keep as a Reference	Read and Pass on to Friends	Throw Out	Don't Receive
• *Member News*	1 ☐	2 ☐	3 ☐	4 ☐
• *Calendar of Events*	1 ☐	2 ☐	3 ☐	4 ☐

(The following are available to Subscriber or higher level members.)

	Keep as a Reference	Read and Pass on to Friends	Throw Out	Don't Receive
• *Garden Gazette*	1 ☐	2 ☐	3 ☐	4 ☐
• *Great Gardening Series* handbooks	1 ☐	2 ☐	3 ☐	4 ☐

8. What newsletter article topics do you like?
(Please check one box for each topic)

	Like a Lot	Like Somewhat	Do Not Like
• Indoor gardening	1 ☐	2 ☐	3 ☐
• Outdoor gardening	1 ☐	2 ☐	3 ☐
• Horticultural personalities	1 ☐	2 ☐	3 ☐
• Reviews of products and publications	1 ☐	2 ☐	3 ☐
• Garden education programs	1 ☐	2 ☐	3 ☐
• Garden staff profiles	1 ☐	2 ☐	3 ☐
• Garden activities	1 ☐	2 ☐	3 ☐
• Garden member profiles	1 ☐	2 ☐	3 ☐

9. **In the past 12 months, how often did you visit the Garden?**
   - 1 ☐ 1 time
   - 2 ☐ 2–4 times
   - 3 ☐ 5+ times
   - 4 ☐ Did not visit

10. **How often do you attend Member-only events?**
   - 1 ☐ Almost always
   - 2 ☐ Several times a year
   - 3 ☐ Occasionally
   - 4 ☐ Not at all

11. **If you attend Member-only events, please tell us why? If you do not attend, please skip to the next question.**
   (Please check all that apply)
   - 1 ☐ It sounds interesting and/or fun when I hear or read about the event
   - 2 ☐ I enjoy the exclusivity of the events—just for us
   - 3 ☐ I like the ambiance of the event
   - 4 ☐ It's a good outing with family and friends
   - 5 ☐ Other *(please specify):* _____

12. **If you do not attend Member-only events, please tell us why:**
   (Please check all that apply)
   - 1 ☐ The events are not held at convenient times
   - 2 ☐ The events didn't sound interesting and/or fun
   - 3 ☐ The events are too crowded
   - 4 ☐ I'm not sure when events are scheduled
   - 5 ☐ Other *(please specify):* _____

13. How do you feel your membership is priced?

¹ ☐ Too low   ² ☐ Just right   ³ ☐ Too high

14. If your membership dues increased, how much more would you be willing to pay?

¹ ☐ $10   ³ ☐ $20

² ☐ $15   ⁴ ☐ I wouldn't pay any increase

15. Are you planning to renew your membership?

¹ ☐ Yes   ² ☐ No   ³ ☐ I haven't decided yet

16. If not, please tell us why: _____

_____

17. If you are no longer a member, please tell us why:

¹ ☐ Didn't use membership benefits

² ☐ Could no longer afford my membership

³ ☐ Not satisfied with Garden facilities or exhibits

⁴ ☐ Not satisfied with membership services

⁵ ☐ No longer interested in the Garden

⁶ ☐ Left the immediate area

⁷ ☐ Never got my renewal notice

⁸ ☐ Other (*please specify*): _____

18. **Have you ever visited the Garden's Web site?**

   1 ☐ Yes   2 ☐ No

19. **How interesting do you find the following areas of the Web site?**
   (Please check one box for each topic)

	Very Interesting	Somewhat Interesting	Not Too Interesting
• Activities at the Garden	1 ☐	2 ☐	3 ☐
• What's in Bloom at the Garden	1 ☐	2 ☐	3 ☐
• Tips for Your Garden	1 ☐	2 ☐	3 ☐
• Book Reviews	1 ☐	2 ☐	3 ☐
• Plants of the Northeast	1 ☐	2 ☐	3 ☐
• Plant Contests	1 ☐	2 ☐	3 ☐

20. **Would a Member-only section of our Web site be of interest to you?**

   1 ☐ Yes   2 ☐ No

21. **Which of the following organizations do you belong to?**
   (Please check all that apply)

   1 ☐ Metro Botanical Garden
   2 ☐ Metro Zoo
   3 ☐ Audubon Society
   4 ☐ American Horticultural Society
   5 ☐ Horticultural Alliance of the Northeast
   6 ☐ Metro Horticultural Society
   7 ☐ The Garden Conservancy
   8 ☐ Planting Fields Arboretum
   9 ☐ Green Guerillas
   10 ☐ Metro Museum of Art

22. Do you subscribe to any of the following publications?
(Please check all that apply)

1 ☐ Horticulture
2 ☐ Fine Gardening
3 ☐ Gardens Illustrated
4 ☐ Herb Companion
5 ☐ Martha Stewart Living
6 ☐ Garden Design

7 ☐ Green Scene (Pennsylvania Horticultural Society)
8 ☐ Country Journal
9 ☐ Organic Gardening
10 ☐ House & Garden
11 ☐ Other (please specify): _____

23. Are you
1 ☐ Under 25
2 ☐ 25–35
3 ☐ 36–45
4 ☐ 46–54

5 ☐ 55–64
6 ☐ 65–74
7 ☐ 75+

24. Are you
1 ☐ Male
2 ☐ Female

25. Do you have children?
1 ☐ Yes
2 ☐ No (If no, skip to Question 27.)

26. **If yes, how many children do you have in each of the following age groups:**

	1 Child	2 Children	3 Children	4 Children or More
• 0–6 years old	1 ☐	2 ☐	3 ☐	4 ☐
• 7–12 years old	1 ☐	2 ☐	3 ☐	4 ☐
• 13–18 years old	1 ☐	2 ☐	3 ☐	4 ☐
• Over 18	1 ☐	2 ☐	3 ☐	4 ☐

27. **What is your primary residence?**
   1 ☐ House or townhouse   2 ☐ Apartment

   Do you:
   3 ☐ Own   4 ☐ Rent

28. **Do you have an outdoor gardening space?**
   1 ☐ Yes   2 ☐ No

29. **If yes, what kind?**
   (*Please check all that apply*)
   1 ☐ Backyard   4 ☐ Community garden
   2 ☐ Container   5 ☐ Country home
   3 ☐ Terrace or roof

30. **What is your zip code?** ___ ___ ___

31. **What is your annual household income before taxes?**
    1 ☐ Below $14,999
    2 ☐ $15,000–$29,999
    3 ☐ $30,000–$49,999
    4 ☐ $50,000–$74,999
    5 ☐ $75,000–$99,999
    6 ☐ $100,000–$199,999
    7 ☐ $200,000+

32. **What is the highest level of formal education you have completed?**
    1 ☐ Some high school
    2 ☐ High school degree
    3 ☐ Some college
    4 ☐ College degree
    5 ☐ Graduate or doctoral degree

Thank you very much for participating in this survey.

Introduction

Although a cover letter should always accompany the mail questionnaire, the questionnaire should include an introductory paragraph that serves the same purpose as the cover letter (in case the two are separated). It should motivate the respondent to fill out the form and give instructions for returning it.

Coded Answers

The small number by each answer box is there to help the data entry person input the data more efficiently and accurately. It is these numbers that are entered and not the longer verbal answers. This practice of *coding* responses makes data entry much quicker and more accurate.

Conclusion

This chapter has provided samples of two complete actual questionnaires that illustrate the implementation of the four principles of questionnaire design. Happy questionnaire writing!

7

Administering the Survey

The guidelines you will follow when administering your survey will vary depending upon the survey methodology you are using. Therefore this chapter discusses key implementation procedures for the four main methodologies:

- Mail surveys
- Telephone surveys
- In-person interviews
- Internet surveys

Administering the Mail Survey

Generally the mail survey package includes a cover letter, the questionnaire, a business reply envelope (BRE), and of course an outer envelope. Let's discuss each in turn.

The Cover Letter

The cover letter may be printed either on the nonprofit's stationery or the research vendor's. It is usually best, as discussed earlier, for the cover letter to be from the nonprofit's chief executive or from whomever at the nonprofit the constituents are most likely to desire to respond to. Once again, the main purpose of the cover letter is to maximize response, because the higher the response rate, the more valid the results will be. Encouraging a good rate of response is an especially critical factor in designing mail surveys because they are infamous for having unsatisfactory response rates unless something additional, such as reminder postcards or phone calls, is done to prompt people to respond.

There are two reasons why people are more likely to respond when the survey cover letter comes from the nonprofit. First, the recipient is much more likely to feel some affinity when it is the nonprofit rather than a research organization that requests help. Second, when the cover letter is from a representative of the nonprofit and on the nonprofit's letterhead, it lends the survey more credibility than it would otherwise have. It can then be seen as authorized by the nonprofit.

There are advantages to a cover letter that comes from an outside research agency. It can instill a feeling in the respondent that her answers are confidential, and it can be used to obtain the answers in a partially blind and therefore more objective fashion because it can state that the nonprofit will not see any individual answers. An additional brief letter from an executive of the nonprofit on the organization's letterhead can tell the respondent that a research firm has been hired to improve the quality of the results as well as to maintain confidentiality. This letter can be sent before the questionnaire or be included with it.

Often, however, the need for a high response rate outweighs any benefits the nonprofit might obtain from encouraging respondents to see the survey as confidential. The exception usually occurs when small nonprofits are conducting surveys, and the organization's donors and executives might know each other. In this case the promise of confidentiality might increase the response.

The Questionnaire

The survey instrument itself, prepared as discussed in the previous chapters, is usually best presented in booklet form, rather than as several sheets stapled together. As mentioned earlier, the four-page booklet is constructed from 11-by-17-inch paper folded once to make four 8½-by-11-inch pages. If an eight-page questionnaire is desired, nest two of the 11-by-17-inch folded sheets, and staple them on the crease, with at least one staple at the top and one at the bottom.

Given the importance of maximizing response, it is critical that the design of the questionnaire be attractive. It should incorporate a lot of white space and use a font size of at least 10 points. Moreover, the font size should increase as the age of the recipients increases. For example, if the average age of the respondents is expected to be sixty years or more, the font size should not be less than 12 points.

Using a second color will give the questionnaire more visual variety, and this will likely increase the response rate. Even if your nonprofit decides a second color will probably not be cost effective, the questionnaire can still be attractively designed through good use of white space and of italics, bold, and other emphases. A questionnaire that looks unprofessionally designed may cause the recipient to feel that his time is not considered very important and lower the likelihood of response.

The Outer Envelope

Other than to transport the contents, the primary purpose of the outer envelope is to motivate the constituent to open it. Because nonprofits are well known for sending financial solicitations and because a large portion of these are thrown away without being opened, it is critical that the outer envelope of your survey look different from a solicitation envelope.

Several tactics will increase the likelihood that the respondent will open the envelope. First, use first-class postage. Many people look at the postage paid by the sender to determine whether the contents are so-called junk mail, and then they open or throw away the envelope accordingly. Also, it is best to use a postage stamp rather than a postage meter. The latter looks less personal and therefore motivates fewer people to open the envelope. Second, the address should look personally applied. Instead of using adhesive-backed mailing labels, it's best to print the addresses using a laser or ink-jet printer. Finally, if your nonprofit sends a lot of solicitations to the population being surveyed (donors, for example) and if it will be mentioning that a research firm is assisting with the survey, consider mailing the questionnaire in the research firm's envelope. The firm's name is likely to be new to the respondent and not associated with either junk mail or solicitations, and the envelope will look personalized with first-class postage and quality addressing so it will almost certainly be opened. Even when you are using a research firm's outer envelope, the cover letter should in almost all cases still be from the leader of the nonprofit on the nonprofit's stationery.

The Reply Envelope

Because maximizing the mail survey response rate is so critical, a business reply envelope must be included in the survey package. It should be preaddressed, with return postage paid. Remember that you are asking the respondent to invest up to thirty minutes completing the survey, which may be costly to him. If he sees that you are not even willing to spend a few cents for a reply envelope, he may feel that responding would not be a good use of his time.

It is generally most cost effective to use a business reply account rather than actual stamps on this reply envelope. The postage is thus free to the constituent, and the Postal Service charges you only for the mail actually returned. Affixing actual stamps to envelopes that may not be returned is unnecessarily expensive. In addition, research has shown that nonprofit constituents are often offended by this use of stamps, feeling it is a poor use of donated funds.

When a research firm is being identified as assisting the nonprofit, it may be worthwhile to address the BRE to that firm. Not only is this more efficient in terms of getting the completed surveys to the researcher but it can support any statements the cover letter makes about the confidentiality of people's answers. However, if you feel that your donors may take offense at research firm involvement (as is often the case with older people), it will be best to address the BRE to the nonprofit and then pass the completed surveys along in one or two installments (see Chapter Two) to the research firm.

Identifying Members of Subgroups

As previously mentioned, it is often informative to sample one or more key subgroups when conducting a survey. It is fairly easy to keep track of which completed questionnaires are from which sub-group when surveying is done by phone or in person. This tracking is more complicated for mail surveys. However, when you have only a few subgroups to keep track of (for example, current versus lapsed or large versus small donors), it might be cost effective to print questionnaires on two or more colors of paper and assign one color to each subgroup. Questionnaires can then be easily told apart for coding and analysis when they are returned.

In many cases the best tracking strategy is to include some key characteristics that define the subgroups on each respondent's questionnaire. For example, if you wish to analyze people's answers in relation to their giving characteristics, you might use these characteristics: the number of years since the first gift, the date of the last gift, the largest gift size, and membership status. This information is pulled from your database and entered into the research data. Ideally, coding representing this information for each respondent is printed on a panel of the questionnaire that shows on the outside when the questionnaire is folded. If it is printed on the bottom of the last page, for example, then the questionnaire can be *fan-folded*, so that the top of the front page shows on one side of the folded document and the bottom of the back page shows on the other side. The outer envelopes are also coded. Then the people stuffing the envelopes can regularly confirm that the correct questionnaire is going to the correct person. Possibly the best place to place the coded information on the outer envelope is on a line above the name, shifted to the far right of the address area. (The code cannot be placed under the state and zip code line because it will interfere with Postal Service scanners.) If the questionnaire is printed on a laser printer, the unique coding at the bottom of each questionnaire is easily facilitated by a software program. If it is not possible to print the coding electronically, hand coding will also work. The accuracy of the hand coding is likely to be higher when the envelopes are coded first and the worker records the code directly from the addressed envelope onto a questionnaire and then immediately stuffs that questionnaire into that envelope.

Administering the Telephone Survey

There are five basic topics to consider when conducting a survey by phone: (1) whether or not to use CATI (computer-assisted telephone interviewing) software, and (2) selecting, (3) training, (4) monitoring, and (5) motivating interviewers. Let's discuss these in order.

Computer-Assisted Telephone Interviewing

As it has with many tasks in the work environment, the computer has revolutionized the way telephone surveys are conducted. With CATI, every interviewer works at a computer terminal. The questionnaire appears on the screen, and the interviewer records the answers using the computer keyboard. Of course it is still possible to conduct surveys using paper and pencil, but there are great advantages to employing computer technology, as the following discussion illustrates.

Easier Handling of Complicated Skip Patterns. Depending on your informational needs and the number of your subgroups, complicated skip patterns may be helpful. For example, an organization recently asked my firm to conduct a survey so that its staff could get information they needed to improve some curricula they had developed. However, the respondents had many varied experiences with these curricula, so not all questions were relevant for each respondent. Determining which questions were relevant required tracking each respondent's previous answers.

When just two or three simple skips are required, a paper-and-pencil questionnaire is workable. However, when there are many skips or when they are complicated, as they would be in the example, the interviewer may get confused and read the wrong questions occasionally. Additionally, her confusion could become obvious to the respondent, increasing the likelihood that the interview will fail. CATI can handle even the most complicated skip patterns flawlessly and bring the appropriate question up on the interviewer's monitor. It can decide whether or not to ask a question based on the combined answers to several previous questions and on other information on the calling list such as member type, recency of last gift, and size of largest gift.

Simpler Tracking of Sampling Quotas. Let's say that your survey calls for one hundred interviews among each of four different subgroups (four hundred interviews total), and it is important that each subgroup is at least 50 percent female. If this were tracked manually during the interview process, it would be time consuming and error prone. However, CATI software can keep track of how many of each group have been sampled and bring up on the screen the appropriate person to call to continue completing the sample.

More Efficient Scheduling and Prompting for Callbacks. To maximize the response rate it is critical that the interviewer arrange a callback if the respondent is not able to be interviewed at the time he is initially called. Recording and, especially, remembering to keep these interview appointments is difficult when using paper questionnaires. However, with CATI, these appointments are entered into the computer, and the CATI program brings the appointment (and the respondent's name, telephone number, and other important information) to the attention of whichever interviewer is available at the time of the appointment.

Easier Rotation of Responses and Questions. Studies have shown that people are more likely to remember the first and last items recited from a list than the intervening items. This being the case, always offering the possible responses in the same order will likely introduce bias into the results. CATI software can circumvent this by rotating the response options. Furthermore, the responses can be rotated individually, in the way that is best for each question. For example, you would not want to rotate answer options that are listed in a logical order, as age or income ranges typically are, for example. You would not want responses that form a symmetrical scale, running from very satisfied to very dissatisfied, for example, to be rotated randomly, but they should be rotated top to bottom and bottom to top. Preference responses, such as lists of favored organizations, should be rotated randomly.

It is also helpful to rotate the subquestions in batteries of questions, such as questions 2, 4, 7, 11, 13, 16, and 19 in Exhibit 6.1, because people sometimes pay more attention to the first in a series of questions and answer the remaining ones more disinterestedly. Also, the answers to later subquestions may be affected by the issues raised or words used in one or more of the previous subquestions. Rotating questions helps to neutralize these tendencies.

More Accurate Evaluation of Interviewer Performance. To keep the costs of a telephone survey down, it is important that the researcher keep track of the performance of paid interviewers. With CATI software the researcher can easily learn how many surveys each interviewer completes overall and per hour. She can also learn how long it takes each interviewer to complete the average interview. This will help her to better coach, and discontinue if necessary, the poor performers.

Lower Data Entry Expenses. When paper questionnaires are used, the interviewer records the responses on the questionnaire and a data entry person later keys in all these data for computerized statistical analysis. CATI eliminates the data entry time because the data entry and interviewing occur simultaneously.

There are several companies that produce CATI software. These software packages vary in quality and price. Full systems generally start at $1,500 for one interviewer and range upward as the number of interviewers rises. At the time of this book's printing, a nonexhaustive list included the following vendors. The first vendor's product is priced especially attractively.

Creative Research Systems, Petaluma, Calif. (707) 765-1001

Sawtooth Technologies, Evanston, Ill. (847) 866-0876

Cybernetic Solution Co., Salt Lake City, Utah (801) 568-1190

Ronin, Princeton, N.J. (609) 452-0060

Interviewer Selection

Selecting the appropriate interviewers is critical to the success of a phone survey. The interviewers need to be fluent and articulate in their speech. They must be good readers and able to manage the conversation with the respondent. Some of the constituents called may be hard of hearing. Others may be in a hurry and not want any small talk. Still others will want to give the interviewer their life stories and will need help keeping on track. Some respondents will simply not be capable of taking a survey because they cannot make decisions or give straight answers. These individuals need to be politely thanked and those interviews terminated. Of course, all interviewers need to be polite and not be easily ruffled. They need to have resilient personalities and not be deterred by feelings of rejection after they hear a string of unkind refusals.

An excellent source of interviewers is college or university students. They are usually bright, quick on the uptake, open to part-time or temporary work, and available at very reasonable rates. Be cautious of those with telemarketing experience, however. People who are good at selling over the phone may have difficulty suppressing the traits that make them strong at sales but are less desirable in interviewing, such as talking rapidly, just as a research interviewer who is good at gaining rapport may have difficulty becoming a salesperson.

Prospective telephone interviewers need to be thoroughly interviewed just as you would any prospective employee. Then they need to be trained.

Interviewer Training

Proper interviewer training will make the difference between accurate and inaccurate results. Here are some tips to consider. Interviewers should practice before getting on the phones. They should read the questionnaire several times through, perhaps rehearsing the interview with another caller. As they do this, questions will usually come up. It is best for the supervisor or researcher to answer these questions with all interviewers present. Not only is this the most efficient use of everyone's time but it ensures that each interviewer receives the same instructions.

Train the interviewers to read the questions verbatim. This ensures that all respondents are communicating the same concepts. Interviewers should understand that changing the wording just slightly can change the meaning of the questions from the perspective of the respondent.

Have the interviewers obtain permission even for changes to the introduction. My colleagues and I allow interviewers a little personal variation when reading the introduction, but we want to know what they are changing before they change it. The primary goal of the introduction is to convert the cold call into a completed interview. As part of this process, it is critical that the interviewer make a smooth, comfortable, positive impression on the respondent, and changing the introduction slightly may help an interviewer do that. Nevertheless, critical aspects of the introduction should not be changed, such as information about whether the survey is blind, about the sponsoring organization, and about the purpose of the survey. Of course it is acceptable to change some words, such as saying "good afternoon" rather than "hello."

Next, interviewers must be trained never to interpret the answers they hear. Respondents frequently do not answer the questions as asked. For example, an interviewer might ask, "How often do you feel you receive mail from XYZ University: more often than you like, about the right amount, or less often than you like?" and it would not be unusual for the respondent to say, "Well, it's not too bad." The untrained interviewer might naturally interpret that to mean about the right amount, mark the questionnaire accordingly, and proceed to the next question. The trained interviewer will gently guide the respondent to answer only from the available choices. For example, he might respond by saying, "OK, so would that be more often than you like, about the right amount, or less often than you like?" You might be surprised at how often the respondent will then come back with a different choice from the one the interviewer anticipated.

Interviewer Monitoring

To ensure the best quality it is necessary to monitor the interviewers as they work. Even though much can be learned simply by standing next to a caller while she is on the phone, the most accurate means of monitoring is random and remote, using a telephone system feature designed for this purpose. All the supervisor needs to do is enter the interviewer's extension on her telephone keypad, and she can monitor the conversation without the respondent's hearing any distracting *splash* sounds.

Monitoring is important because it allows the researcher to learn how smoothly and accurately the questionnaire is being read, how accurately answers are being recorded, and the degree to which respondents might be pleased or annoyed with a caller.

Finally, please note that some states require that the respondent be informed if his or her call may be monitored. To comply with this regulation, you may need to insert a sentence such as this into the introduction: "To ensure quality, this call may be monitored."

Interviewer Motivation

Your nonprofit can save substantial time and money by keeping its callers properly motivated. One strategy is to offer a base rate of pay plus a bonus for each survey completed. Another very effective and possibly less costly method is simply to post how many interviews each caller has conducted in total and per hour. It is not unusual for these incentives to increase productivity by 50 to 100 percent. However, when incentives are offered, monitoring becomes even more critical for accurate evaluation of the callers' progress and quality. Unfortunately, some callers may cheat by falsifying questionnaires.

Administering the In-Person Interview

The guidelines for administering an in-person interview depend on where the interview will be conducted. For the interview in a person's home or office (sometimes desirable for major donor interviews), the director or some other executive at the nonprofit should send a letter respectfully requesting the individual's participation. The letter should inform the person of the survey's basic purpose and approximate length and emphasize the importance of his input. It should also indicate that the interviewer or another person will call in a certain number of days to schedule the interview. For central location surveys, for which respondents come to the interviewer, the recruiting and screening of respondents is generally done by phone.

Once the in-person interview has been scheduled, conducting it is very similar to telephone interviewing. Many of the same guidelines apply. Even computer-assisted interviewing is available. The questions are shown on the screen, and the interviewer simply records the answers using the keyboard or asks the respondent to do so. The software for this is called CAPI, or computer-assisted personal interviewing.

Personal interview studies are usually very expensive. Recruiting costs alone can rival the costs of conducting a phone survey, and for central location studies a substantial monetary incentive is generally required to motivate people to come to the research site. A nonprofit should have a compelling reason for using this methodology, such as needing to field exceptionally long or complex studies with which respondents may need special assistance, needing to use numerous visual examples, or needing to exercise special security measures. Because of the cost of in-person interviewing and the difficulty of obtaining a valid sample and adequate response rate, further discussion is beyond the scope of this book.

Administering the Internet Survey

The key thing to keep in mind when your nonprofit wishes to use an Internet survey is how sampling and response rates affect validity. Internet surveys are not usually considered valid, because typically researchers can reach only a small portion of their target population through the Internet. An exception to this stipulation is the survey that asks Web site visitors to evaluate the Web site. The entire population of interest, that is, 100 percent of the visitors, is available to be sampled. The challenge then is to maximize response rate by getting the largest portion possible to respond. Oftentimes it is necessary to offer incentives, such as money or free products. Many of the telephone procedures related in this chapter are applicable to Internet interviews. Because of the rarity of this procedure at the present time, further discussion is beyond the scope of this book. However, those with a particular interest in online surveys may wish to take a look at the Council of American Survey Research Organizations' Web page of frequently asked questions about conducting on-line research [www.casro.org/faq/faq1099.htm] for some Internet surveying principles.

Conclusion

Each of the four main means of administering surveys—by mail, by telephone, in person, and on the Internet—has important ramifications for the response rate and therefore the validity of the results. Generally, a phone survey will offer the best balance between cost effectiveness and validity of results although there are some circumstances in which one of the other means may be preferable.

8

Analyzing the Survey Results

Describing how to analyze survey data could require many volumes, and in fact, many volumes have been written about it. My purpose here is not to provide comprehensive instruction but simply to present some highlights of the process and help you differentiate those aspects that you might wish a professional to undertake and those that could be undertaken in house. The chapter looks first at some software packages and then discusses types of statistical analysis.

Survey Software Packages

Whether your survey is conducted by mail or by phone, you will want to use a computer for data entry and statistical analysis. Some of the relevant computer software is designed only for survey data entry and statistical analysis, whereas other packages also offer the CATI (computer-assisted telephone interviewing) option. Still others offer only CATI and not statistical analysis. Some software packages are also capable of formatting the questionnaire that you type in.

Currently, Stat-Pac is an example of relatively inexpensive (about $1,000) software that was designed specifically for survey analysis and is strong in statistics but does not offer full CATI. The Survey System offers a full range of CATI and statistical analysis features and costs from $500 to $1,500+, depending on the volume and quality of interviewing you would like to be able to do. SPSS (Statistical Package for the Social Sciences) and SAS are general statistical packages that can be used for survey data entry and analysis but are not designed specifically for them. You can not use them to format a questionnaire (except through separate modules), nor do they have CATI functions unless used in conjunction with other products.

Unfortunately, most survey software packages are designed for professional survey researchers and statisticians. As such, they are very complex, and they rarely explain the meanings of statistical algorithms and when to use each type. To obtain the most value from their data, it is likely that the vast majority of nonprofits will need to obtain the services of a professional researcher in this stage of the survey.

Nonprofits that cannot afford a professional researcher sometimes use spreadsheet packages, such as Microsoft Excel. These can perform the most simple analysis, referred to as frequency analysis, which is discussed later. Many spreadsheets offer a broad array of data analysis capabilities, including several statistical procedures and tests. They also are able to produce some good graphs. Accessing the analytical power of a spreadsheet can be time and labor intensive, however. Because spreadsheets are so flexible, users have to specify the location and structure of the data, the type of analysis desired, and the appropriate commands to do the analysis. This once again presupposes a strong base of analytical knowledge and experience. Still, those who regularly use spreadsheets should be able to navigate their way through some basic descriptive analysis, such as frequency analysis.

Another option is to use off-the-shelf database packages, such as Microsoft Access. These do not provide the analytical power of statistical software or even of spreadsheets; however, they are useful for creating forms to assist in data entry and improve its speed and accuracy. Organizations with staff members well versed in both database packages and spreadsheets may wish to enter the data in a database program, then export data tables to a spreadsheet for analysis.

Once you have selected your software package(s), and set up a questionnaire template for data entry, data entry may proceed. Often these packages offer security features that prevent the data entry person from mistakenly entering nonapplicable data. For example, if a question asks for the respondent's gender, the data entry screen can be programmed to accept only "M" or "F" as data; any other entries will be rejected, and the data entry person will be asked to insert a correct answer. Many professional researchers have the data entered twice. They then use advanced software to compare the two data files for consistency. This allows many data entry errors to be identified and corrected.

Statistical Analyses

This section offers an overview of frequency analysis, cross-tabulation analysis, banners analysis, and analysis to determine statistical significance. It also addresses the analysis of answers to open-ended questions and the graphic presentation of statistical results.

Frequency Analysis

The first step in the statistical analysis of a survey is to run a *frequency analysis*. The frequency analysis simply shows the frequency with which respondents gave each of the possible answers to each question. Because the absolute number of people responding with each answer is usually not that important, this statistical procedure displays the percentage results.

Frequency analysis is an easy routine, and the computer software should do it more or less instantaneously. The results should display how many people responded to each answer for each question and the number of entered questionnaires on which there was no response to the question, sometimes referred to as *missing cases*. In addition, the software is likely to offer an option to calculate the confidence interval for each percentage result.

Those using Excel or another spreadsheet for data analysis will find the "frequency" function useful for creating simple frequency tables. It not only counts the number of times a specified value occurs in a column or other array but also offers the option of grouping responses into categories (for example, if respondents have provided their exact ages, it can sort them into ranges like 40–49, 50–59, and so on). Table 8.1 is an example of a frequency analysis for one question.

One thing to note in the analysis in Table 8.1 is that the confidence interval, or estimate of error (defined in Chapter Three), varies depending on how close the percentage of respondents selecting a particular response to a question is to 50 percent or to the extremes of 0 percent and 100 percent. The closer it is to 50 percent, the wider the confidence interval. The closer the percentage is to 0 percent or 100 percent, the narrower the confidence interval.

Table 8.2 contains a chart for determining the confidence intervals for answers to questions depending on how close they are to 50 percent or to 0 percent and 100 percent and on how large the survey's sample is. First, find the column heading that is closest to your sample size. Next, find the row for the percentage result closest to that found for the particular answer to a question that you are

TABLE 8.1 Frequency Analysis for One Question.

	Frequency	Percentage	Confidence Interval (At 95% Level)
1. Very well	66	24	± 5.2%
2. Somewhat well	129	47	± 5.5
3. Not too well	48	18	± 4.6
4. Not at all well	30	11	± 3.8
Total	273	100	
Missing cases	11		
Total cases	284		

interested in. The cell at the intersection of the row and column displays the confidence interval, or estimate of error, plus and minus. Adding and subtracting this percentage from the observed result generally produces a range within which there is a 95% chance that the answer is valid for the group being sampled.

This procedure can be reversed to help you determine the sample size you need for your next survey. The best way to do this is to determine, based on your judgment and experience, the largest range of error you will be comfortable with (for example, ±5%). Next find that range in the 50 percent row. Then look at the column heading for the sample size you will need (in this case, four hundred).

Note that this discussion relates to the accuracy of general survey results. When comparing the results of two subgroups, such as current versus lapsed donors, a different procedure is followed and usually requires a larger sample size.

Frequency analysis will work with most of your survey results; however, some recoding may be necessary. For example, if your questionnaire included an age question with no predefined ranges, so that each respondent's actual age was entered directly, then the frequency analysis would list out the results for every age. For example, if people of every age between eighteen and ninety responded to the survey, the frequency analysis would list out each of the seventy-three ages in that range and the number and percentage of respondents for each age. Such data are rather unwieldy to analyze, and the researcher may first wish to recode the individual ages into ranges containing five or ten years each.

Cross-Tabulation Analysis

A frequently used and beneficial statistical technique is the *cross-tabulation analysis*. This determines how many people responding to a particular answer for one question also responded to a particular answer for a second question. The process is repeated multiple times so that each answer for one question is examined in relation to all the answers for the other question. For example, if a researcher ran

TABLE 8.2 Confidence Intervals for Specific Survey Responses.

Percentage Result for a Specific Response	Sample Size										
	100	200	300	400	500	600	800	1,000	1,500	3,000	5,000
5% or 95%	4.4	3.1	2.5	2.2	2.0	1.8	1.5	1.4	1.1	0.79	0.62
10% or 90%	6.0	4.3	3.5	3.0	2.7	2.5	2.1	2.0	1.6	1.1	0.85
15% or 85%	7.1	5.1	4.1	3.6	3.2	2.9	2.5	2.3	1.9	1.3	1.0
20% or 80%	8.0	5.7	4.6	4.0	3.6	3.3	2.6	2.5	2.1	1.4	1.1
25% or 75%	8.7	6.1	5.0	4.3	3.9	3.6	3.0	2.8	2.3	1.6	1.2
30% or 70%	9.2	6.5	5.3	4.6	4.1	3.8	3.2	2.8	2.4	1.7	1.3
35% or 65%	9.5	6.8	5.5	4.8	4.3	3.9	3.3	3.1	2.5	1.7	1.4
40% or 60%	9.8	7.0	5.7	4.9	4.4	4.0	3.4	3.1	2.5	1.8	1.4
45% or 55%	9.9	7.0	5.8	5.0	4.5	4.1	3.5	3.2	2.6	1.8	1.4
50%	10.0	7.1	5.8	5.0	4.5	4.1	3.5	3.2	2.6	1.8	1.4

Source: B. Campbell, "Improving Fund Raising Via Donor Surveys," *Fund Raising Management,* July 1992, p. 44–46.

a cross-tabulation analysis of age against income, she might find that people aged fifty-six to sixty-five are likely to have a higher median household income (for example, $50,000) than those aged forty-six to fifty-five (whose median household income is $42,000) and those aged sixty-six to seventy-five years (whose median household income is $32,500). Or a researcher might run a question about the reasons people discontinue donating against a question about gender to find out if females tend to discontinue for different reasons than males do. Table 8.3 is an example of what this cross-tabulation analysis might find: it indicates that males are more likely to discontinue donating because they do not have the money and females are more likely to discontinue because they are giving to another charity.

Banners Analysis

The *banners analysis* is an extension of the cross-tab analysis but is much more comprehensive. Instead of comparing the responses to two questions, the banners analysis typically compares all the answers to most if not all of the questions in a survey with the answers to each of three to six key questions.

The analysis results are set up as a table, in which the columns headings (called *banner points*) are the possible responses (or range of responses) to each key question, and the row labels (called *stubs*) are possible responses to other survey questions (as many as desired, but usually a majority of those in the survey). In a typical analysis there are twelve to eighteen banner points. The answers chosen for the banner points typically address demographics, such as gender, age, income, and the like, but might also include several other key

TABLE 8.3 Cross-Tabulation Analysis.

Reasons for Discontinuing	Females	Males	Total
Don't have the money	20%	80%	100%
Giving to another charity	70	30	100

questions. For example, if you were conducting a readership survey, you might wish to include banner points for low and high readership so that you could see whether these two groups differed in their responses to the survey questions. As in Table 8.3, the percentages (and often the actual counts) of the people providing each answer are displayed in the table cells. The result is a vast array of comparisons, as illustrated in Table 8.4.

Analyses to Determine Whether the Difference Between Two Results Is Coincidental or Reflects a True Difference in the Population

Frequently, an executive would like to know whether the difference in the responses of two subgroups to a question is more likely to be a true difference or to have happened by chance. For example, consider a survey of current and lapsed donors. If there is a true difference between the way these groups responded to a key question, it might suggest that the nonprofit should communicate differently

TABLE 8.4 Banner Analysis.

Question: Which features of the ABC Nonprofit's monthly newsletter do you like the most?

	Gender		Age		Income		Largest Donation	
	Male	Female	<40	50+	<$30K	$50K+	<$99	$200+
President's column	25%	75%	35%	30%	25%	20%	10%	10%
Cover article	10	10	15	40	25	30	5	50
Readers respond	10	5	20	20	25	30	35	20
Schedule of events	55	10	30	10	25	20	50	20
Totals	100	100	100	100	100	100	100	100

with each one. There are a number of statistical tests that will determine the likelihood that a difference might have occurred by chance. These tests take into account (1) the sample sizes of the two groups, (2) the percentages of the groups giving the responses, (3) the size of the difference between the responses, and (4) the total population size. The *difference of proportions* test, the *difference of means test,* and the *chi-square* test are used most often. The formulas for these tests can be found in most any statistics book, but they require an in-depth understanding of statistics and computer software to run them, which an organization may or may not have in house, and this is likely to be an instance in which outside help would be particularly useful.

Statistical software, whether general purpose or designed specifically for surveys, will be able to run these tests. Typically, tests are run for all of the possible comparisons. Those comparisons found to represent *statistically significant* differences, that is, the ones likely not to have happened by chance, are marked by the computer with an asterisk or similar character. This testing capability is exceptionally helpful when the nonprofit is interested in how the various constituent groups such as high versus low income, high versus low education, or large versus small givers feel about the issues the survey was intended to examine.

Analysis of Numeric Questions

A question that seeks a raw number, such as age (as discussed earlier) or income, is often best evaluated without the use of percentages. For example, it may be best to indicate the range of the answers and give some indication of their typical size. To state this typical size, three options are used the vast majority of the time: mean, median, and mode. The *mean* is the simple arithmetical average: one adds all the answers and divides them by the total number of answers. This is often the way in which the typical age of a population is communicated. The *median* refers to the number that is right at the middle when the numeric answers are listed from highest to lowest. The median is usually the statistic of choice for communicating the typical income of a group, because the mean income is likely to be skewed by the fact that a few people have very high incomes, causing the typical income to look higher than it really is. The *mode* refers to the numeric answer that was provided most often. For example, if a question asked what people felt was the highest donation they would likely make to the nonprofit, the donation size cited most frequently would be the mode.

To calculate these measures (and several more), Excel users may wish to experiment with the "Descriptive Statistics" tool (click on "Tools," then "Data Analysis," then "Descriptive Statistics").

Analysis of Open-Ended Questions

The analysis of open-ended questions is much more laborious than that of closed-ended questions. After all, the number of possible responses for open-ended questions is infinite. Because of the difficulty in analyzing open-ended questions, the researcher usually tries to minimize the number of open-ended questions at the questionnaire design stage. Even so, sometimes the use of open-ended questions is warranted. Here, briefly, is how they are handled in the analysis process.

First, the researcher needs to review a healthy number of the responses to an open-ended question (one hundred or so) in order to create a manageable number of categories. For example, after reviewing one hundred responses to the open-ended question, How can the ABC Nonprofit improve its services? the researcher might identify five to ten categories that together will accommodate all the responses. For example, the categories might be

1. Decrease the frequency of mailings
2. Improve other aspects of communications (for example, the newsletter)
3. Improve membership benefits
4. Improve financial accountability
5. Miscellaneous

Then the researcher or a trained and experienced data entry person needs to classify each response to this question on all the completed surveys in one of these categories. When this process is completed, the responses to the open-ended question can be analyzed using the frequency, cross-tabulation, or banners analyses that were discussed in the previous sections or any number of other more sophisticated analyses (see Resource B).

Graphic Analysis

In analyzing statistical results it is often the case that differences, patterns, or trends become much more apparent when one views them graphically as compared to simply looking at the numbers. For this reason graphs are becoming an expected, if not mandatory, part of any formal survey research report. Moreover, when results are presented in graphic form, the readers are much more likely to meditate on them longer and better assimilate them into an understanding of the subject. This in turn increases the value of the research project. For the same reason, as part of his own analysis of the results, the researcher would do well to graph them first.

This section illustrates some basic graphic tools. Because some sets of results lend themselves more to one type of visual representation than another, I also briefly describe the circumstances under which it might be best to use one type of graph over another.

Pie Graphs

Pie graphs should be used to illustrate relative percentage responses to categorical questions when the results add up to 100 percent or, due to rounding error, very close to that (97 percent to 103 percent). Because most of the questions in the typical survey will be reported in terms of percentages, pie graphs are frequently used. Figure 8.1 shows an example of a pie graph, used in this case to present the gender of respondents.

FIGURE 8.1 Pie Graph.

Gender of Respondent

Male, 31%

Female, 69%

FIGURE 8.2 Bar Graph.

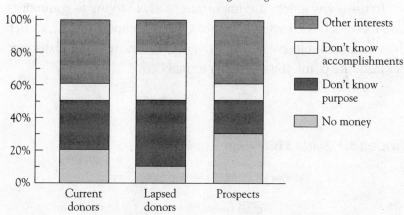

Reasons for Discontinuing Giving

- Other interests
- Don't know accomplishments
- Don't know purpose
- No money

Current donors   Lapsed donors   Prospects

Bar Graphs

Bar graphs are excellent for comparing the results of similar questions or comparing the results of several groups for the same question. For example, if the respondents were asked a battery of questions to elicit how likely they are to discontinue donating for each of a variety of reasons, it would be helpful to use a bar graph to display the percentages of those saying very likely for each reason, as shown in Figure 8.2.

Stacked bar graphs can show more than one response type for each question, for example, both the respondents saying somewhat likely and those saying very likely. An example of a stacked bar graph is provided in Figure 8.3.

Line Graphs

Line graphs are infrequently seen in survey reports because they are best used when the horizontal axis depicts an interval variable, such as time. However, they can be used for age or income to depict a trend, as in Figure 8.4.

   In using any graph, it is important to avoid trying to communicate too much with a single graph. Overly complex graphs, rather than making results clearer, may overwhelm the reader and distract her from the point you are trying to make.

FIGURE 8.3 Stacked Bar Graph.

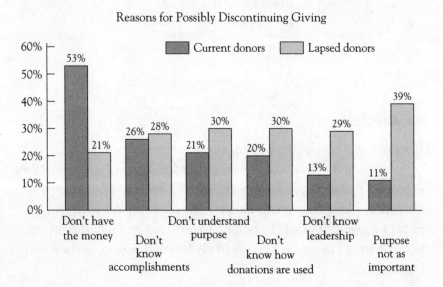

Reasons for Possibly Discontinuing Giving

FIGURE 8.4 Line Graph.

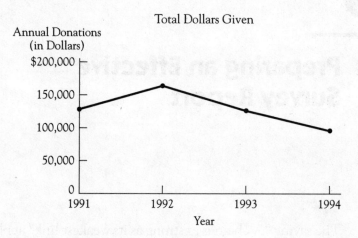

Conclusion

This overview of the most basic aspects of statistical analysis is intended to give the nonprofit executive a better sense of the kinds of statistical information that may be gained from a survey and a realistic understanding of the level of expertise required for getting the most out of his or her investment in conducting the survey.

9

Preparing an Effective Survey Report

The saying "A chain is as strong as its weakest link" applies to the survey report. A nonprofit may invest thousands of dollars and hundreds of hours to obtain the most accurate and helpful information about its constituents. However, if this information is communicated poorly, little of the value will be realized, and the nonprofit will have wasted its time and money. It is critical that the survey report be prepared with the same attention to detail that went into the research itself. Another reason to prepare the report with diligence is that the people looking to the report for information typically cannot see all of the work that went into the research nor ascertain its value. Usually all they see is the report itself, and they may well ascribe a low value to the information if the report is disorganized or unattractive.

This chapter offers guidance in preparing a quality report. It assumes that the analysis, both statistical and conceptual, has been conducted. The only task unfinished is to communicate the results effectively.

The first step is to determine whom the report is for. Is it for the board of directors, the development staff, the executive director, or the vice president of development. Are you the primary user? Of course the level of detail will depend on the audience you are writing for.

Planning the Report Structure

A typical report has the following sections, usually organized in this order (the numbers in parentheses are the typical number of pages in the sections):

Title Page (1)

Table of Contents (1)

Executive Summary (2 to 4)

Introduction (1)

Review of Previous Research (1 to 2)

Methodology (1)

Survey Research Results (1 to 2 per question)

Conclusions (2 to 6)

Appendices (as needed)

Although the report is often *presented* in this order, it is usually better to *write* it in a different order. Most researchers find it most efficient to begin by writing the review of previous research (assuming the nonprofit has conducted earlier research) and then to discuss the survey methodology. Writing these sections first allows the staff or outside researcher to refer to points made in them as she writes the next section, which is the survey research results section, the main body of the report. With the results freshly in mind, the researcher can then write out the report's conclusions. Having discussed the survey results and the conclusions drawn from them, the researcher now has a full picture of what the introduction needs to cover. Therefore the introduction is the next logical section to write. Having written the main body of the report and the introduction, the researcher is now primed to summarize the report, hence the executive summary may be written at this point.

In writing the survey report, the researcher may have found it helpful to reference material or data too long or complex to include in the body of the report. This material can be prepared as appendices at this point. With everything else written, the table of contents should be compiled. The title page may be written at any point.

Writing the Report

The following sections discuss each part of the report in depth, following the writing order just described.

Review of Previous Research

Previous research conducted by the nonprofit on the same topic or topics as the present research should be summarized because comparing it to the current results might aid the reader in better understanding those results and their implications. This section is optional because sometimes there is no previous research. When there is prior research, it is often the qualitative research (focus group or one-on-one depth interviews) conducted just prior to the survey and as part of the same project. This research has usually been explicated in a separate report, and in that case a previous research section is not necessary, but the existence of this qualitative research should be mentioned in the introduction. Sometimes, a survey is one of multiple research efforts designed to reveal changes in people's attitudes over time. In this case the key characteristics of the previous studies (who, what, when) are described in the previous research section and the previous findings are displayed throughout the research results section alongside the current results.

Methodology

The design and the implementation of the research is explained in detail in the methodology section. Although this is usually of little interest to top executives, fellow researchers and more technically oriented staff will want to learn how the study was conducted so they can judge the reliability and validity of the results. In addition, this section will provide documentation that you or someone else in the organization can learn from as you plan future research projects and try to improve your methods.

This section should include a discussion of which sampling frame was used and why, the numbers of people that were sampled from each working population, and the sampling method used. It should also give the specific dates when the fieldwork was conducted, as this may have been some time before the date of the report. Readers often want to know whether the interviews were conducted before or after a particular event.

Another key statistic to include is the response rate, both overall and (preferably) for each subgroup. Additionally, this section should include a discussion of the survey methodology used (telephone, mail, in person, or some other or hybrid method) and the average interview length. Any significant problems that were encountered should also be cited, along with a discussion of any impact these may have had on the accuracy of the results. Sometimes the discussion of the methodology for a simple survey takes only a paragraph or two, so it may be more convenient to include this information in the introduction than to write a methodology section.

Survey Research Results

In the section on the survey results the researcher shares all the findings from the research. There are two main issues to consider here. First, the order in which the results for each question might be discussed, and second, the structure for each question discussion.

One approach to organizing the survey questions for discussion is to arrange them in logical categories. For example, the researcher might start by describing the people interviewed first (listing all the results from demographic questions) and then proceed through the other questions subject area by subject area. For example, a typical donor survey might divide the results into the subject areas of demographics, general perceptions, attitudes regarding communications, and motivations for giving. An alternative method is simply to discuss the questions in the order in which they appear in the questionnaire. This is less time consuming for the researcher, and it has a particular advantage for the report reader. Respondents' answers to later questions may reflect what they learned or thought about as they answered earlier questions on various topics. When the question results are presented in the order of the questionnaire, the report reader has a clear picture of which questions might have influenced, or have been influenced by, other questions. Consider the example of the blind survey. It is sometimes appropriate to interpret the results of a question variously depending on whether or not the name of the sponsoring nonprofit has yet been mentioned to the respondent. When the results are discussed in questionnaire order, the reader knows exactly when the respondent acquired this information.

However, even when the report is ordered in the same manner as the survey, it is helpful to place the demographic results at the beginning for at least two reasons. First, learning who the members of the sample are demographically will help the reader better understand why they hold the attitudes or had the experiences revealed by the survey. Second, because the nondemographic questions usually represent the meat of the study, the demographic results will be anticlimactic if they come last, and they will end the discussion on one of its less interesting notes.

Once a question order has been selected, there are of course a variety of ways to approach the discussions of the individual questions. It will appear most attractive and accessible to the reader if the results from each question on the questionnaire are presented on a separate page (or pages). At the top of each page that starts the discussion of a new question, it is best to print the exact question posed to the respondents. The reader may find it helpful to refer to this question as he ponders the results.

Following the question, the researcher might have a subsection titled "Research Results." This section presents a verbal summary of the actual results obtained for the question and may include graphs and tables. Consider using graphs, as discussed in Chapter Eight, because compared to the typical table of results, graphs do a better job of assisting readers to grasp the results and to compare and contrast them. It is ideal to graph all the basic frequency analysis results. Rarely, however, is it advisable to try to graph every last bit of data. For example, a graph for a question battery that asked how helpful each of several items was and offered the possible responses of *very, somewhat, not too,* or *not at all helpful* might be too cluttered to communicate well. In this case the researcher should decide which results are the most significant to the research objectives and focus on making those clear. For this particular type of question, it is best to graph only the *very helpful* or the combined *very* and *somewhat helpful* responses. Of course when this approach is adopted, the frequency results for the *not too* and *not at all helpful* responses will need to be included somewhere in the report. One way to do this is to graph the most important results, as just described, and then also supply a table with all the results, which the reader may consult if he wishes. Another way, which may increase the readability of the report and avoid overwhelming readers with detail, is to present the less important results only in an appendix that contains a complete listing of all the study findings.

In writing the research results subsection for each question, the researcher would be wise not to offer any interpretation, suggest any implications, make any conclusions, or insert any other subjective matter. It is better to keep this interpretive material in a separate and clearly marked subsection. The thinking here is that it is most helpful to the reader if he knows exactly what is fact and what is opinion. Not everyone will agree on the implications of the survey results, but everyone should be helped to see the indisputable research findings.

Thus the next subsection for each survey question might be the discussion of what the research results mean, including implications, hypotheses, recommendations, and the like. Some possible titles for this section are "Discussion of Results," "Implications," "Communication Considerations," or "Conclusions."

Two examples of typical discussions of question results for two different nonprofits are displayed in Exhibits 9.1 and 9.2. If at all possible the pie and bar graphs and the headings, and also any headers, footers, or borders you might use, would be in color.

EXHIBIT 9.1 University College Research Results.

Question: University College communicates with its donors to inform them about its progress and to request donations. How often do you remember receiving mail from University College that requests donations?

1. More often than you would like
2. About as often as you would like
3. Less often than you would like
4. Don't receive them [**Don't prompt.**]

Research Results

Over half (56%) of the donors felt that University College sends appeals *more often than they like*. Over a third (36%) felt that University College sends appeals *about as often as they like*. Only 5% felt that University College sends appeals *less often than they like*.

Donors with a college degree were more likely to feel that they receive appeals *more often than they like* (68% versus 49%), whereas donors with a graduate degree were more likely to say they receive *about the right amount* (43% versus 27%). Donors who have a family member who attended (46% versus 34%) and those who gave their last gift within the past 12 months (41% versus 31%) were also more likely to feel that University College sends *about the right amount* of mail.

How Often Do You Remember Receiving Appeal Letters?

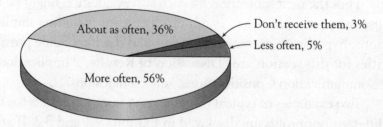

About as often, 36%

Don't receive them, 3%

Less often, 5%

More often, 56%

EXHIBIT 9.1 University College Research Results, Cont'd.

Communications Considerations

Over half (56%) of University College's donors feel they receive mail more often than they like. This is twice as high as the average results found at other institutions of higher education. Another measure to consider is the *more often* versus *less often* ratio. Normally, this ranges from 3:1 to 5:1. At 11.2:1 = 56%:5%), University College's ratio is also much higher. It is hypothesized that the low alumni satisfaction ratings for University College are due at least in part to the tremendous amount of mail the alumni feel they are receiving from the school.

Conclusions

The conclusions section is where the researcher shares the observations and implications derived from the findings, as well as any recommendations, hypotheses to be tested, and further research to be conducted. If conclusions, recommendations, implications, observations, or communication considerations are provided throughout the report in the discussions of the results for individual questions, as described previously, they need only be summarized here.

It is in this section that global observations and trends should be described, along with any concepts that help to weave the separate results into a comprehensive whole, permitting the reader to make the wisest use possible of the survey results.

Introduction

Having written the body of the report, the researcher should have a clear idea of the topics that need to be addressed in the introduction to the report so the reader can make practical use of the information. The introduction is also the place to summarize the reasons why the study was undertaken and to reiterate the primary and

EXHIBIT 9.2 Metro Zoo Research Results.

Question: What other types of organizations do you contribute to?

1. Wildlife (like World Wildlife Fund, National Audubon Society)
2. Environmental (like Environmental Defense Fund, Nature Conservancy, Sierra Club)
3. Children's causes (like UNICEF, Save the Children, Make-A-Wish Foundation)
4. Women's organizations or causes (like Planned Parenthood, National Organization for Women)
5. Local public radio or television

What Other Types of Organizations Do You Contribute To?

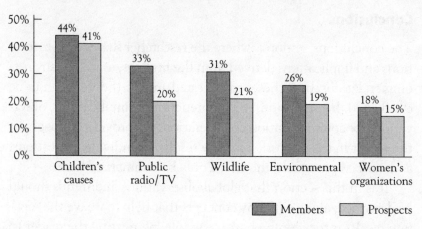

Four out of ten current Metro Zoo members (44%) give to *children's causes* such as UNICEF, Save the Children, and Make-A-Wish Foundation. A third (33%) give to *local public radio or television* and slightly fewer (31%) give to *wildlife* organizations such as World Wildlife Fund and the National Audubon Society. A quarter (26%) give to *environmental* organizations such as the Environmental Defense Fund and the Sierra Club. Less than one in five current members (18%) give to *women's organizations or causes* such as Planned Parenthood or the National Organization for Women.

EXHIBIT 9.2 Metro Zoo Research Results, Cont'd.

Cross-Tabulations

Members who visited Metro Zoo three or more times are more likely than those who visited two or fewer times to donate to *children's causes* (34% versus 25%). Male members are more likely than female members to give to *environmental* organizations (22% versus 16%) and *local public radio or television* (24% versus 19%), whereas female members are more likely to contribute to *children's causes* (33% versus 22%). Members who are 50 years old and older are more likely than members 40 years old and younger to contribute to *environmental* organizations (20% versus 13%) and *local public radio or television* (25% versus 17%). Generally, the younger the member, the more likely he or she is to contribute to *children's causes*.

Members who visited Metro Zoo two or fewer times are more likely than those who visited five or more times to give to *local public radio or television* (25% versus 16%). Members with a high school or professional education are more likely than members with a college degree or advanced degree to give to *children's causes* (37% versus 28%). Family Members are also more likely than One-Plus-One Members to give to *children's causes* (37% versus 25%).

Recommendations

This information can be used to inform member acquisition efforts. For example, mailing lists, such as children's causes lists, may be rented that represent the categories most likely to include members, and presumably, prospective members.

---

maybe some of the secondary objectives that were agreed upon at the start of the project.

Appendices

As mentioned earlier, it is likely that the body of the report will occasionally allude to information that would be helpful to the reader but is too cumbersome to reproduce at that point. This information should be formatted as one or more appendices. Such appendices often include a full copy of the questionnaire, all the frequency results, banner analyses, cross-tabulation analyses, verbatim lists of the responses to open-ended questions, and the like.

Executive Summary

Once the researcher has written just about everything but the table of contents, it is appropriate to write the executive summary. A typical fifteen- to twenty-minute telephone survey might result in a report of seventy pages. Because many people will not have the time to assimilate this much information but would benefit from learning the most critical findings, an executive summary can be a very practical way to disseminate survey findings. It will increase the likelihood that all the work expended and results obtained will be put to use. The summary may be written in a variety of formats. One way is simply to write several pages of summarizing text, using subheadings copiously to help the executive find the information he is looking for quickly. Exhibit 9.3 offers an example of the first section of an executive summary, focusing on the demographics revealed by the survey.

Title Page

The title page is probably the easiest part of the report, but it is still important to take the time to make it attractive, with a pleasing layout and perhaps colors, so that it reflects the quality embedded in the research. The title page should contain the following basic information: (1) the title of the report, (2) the name of the nonprofit for which the survey was conducted, (3) the name of the person or organization responsible for conducting the survey, and (4) the report date (see Exhibit 9.4). Although I have placed the title page toward the end of the list of report sections to write, it may be designed at any point in the process.

EXHIBIT 9.3 Survey Report Executive Summary.

Demographics

The XYZ Health Charity's donors are older, poorer, and more predominantly female than the national donor population. Their median age is 70 (versus the national median of 59) their median household income is $33,000 (versus $39,000), and 66 percent are female (versus 61%). Consistent with this profile, XYZ donors are much more likely to be widowed (26% versus the national norm of 4%) and to have no children under 18 living at home (86% versus the norm of 59%). They are predominantly white (91%, slightly higher than the national donor norm of 87%), with average levels of education (49% completed college versus the national donor norm of 47%).

This demographic profile suggests that gaining new, younger donors will be essential to the XYZ Health Charity in the coming years. It also suggests that among current donors, planned giving should be a key element of the development program.

Gender

The XYZ Health Charity's donors are predominantly female (66% versus 34% male). This is more skewed than both the national population (51% female and 49% male) and the national donor population (61% female and 39% male).

Age

The median age of the respondents is 70 years. Exactly half (50%) of the donors are over 70 years of age. Almost a quarter (23%) are between the ages of 60 and 69, and slightly more than a quarter (27%) are under 60 years of age.

Race

The largest proportion of donors (91%) are Caucasian, which is slightly more than the proportion of donors nationally (87%). Three percent (3%) are Native American. Two percent (2%) are African American, which is less than half the percentage of African American donors nationally (5%). Only 1% are Hispanic, 1% are Asian, and 3% of the donors fell into the "other" category.

EXHIBIT 9.3 Survey Report Executive Summary, Cont'd.

Marital Status

The largest proportion of donors (58%) are married. This is slightly less than the percentage of married people in the general population (61%) and in the U.S. donor population (66%). Ten percent (10%) of the XYZ Health Charity's donors are single, which is almost two-thirds less than the percentage for the national U.S. population (27%), and 7% are divorced, which is the same percentage as in the national U.S. population. However, the XYZ Health Charity's donors are six times more likely to be widowed (26% versus 4%) than the national U.S. population.

Number of Children at Home Under 18

Six out of every seven of the XYZ Health Charity's donors (86%) do not have any children under the age of 18 living in their home. This is significantly higher than the typical U.S. donor percentage of 59%.

Highest Level of Education

The XYZ Health Charity's donors are more than twice as likely (49%) to have completed college or attended graduate school compared with the general U.S. population (21%). Overall, these results are very similar to the national donor population, 47% of which have completed college or attended graduate school.

Household Income

Half (50%) of the respondents, which is a little higher than is normal, did not want to divulge their annual household income. Among those who did, the median income was approximately $33,000. This is slightly lower than the income of the typical U.S. household ($35,000) and considerably lower than that of the typical U.S. donor household ($39,000). Over a quarter (27%) fell in the under $20,000 category. One in five (19%) fell in the $20,000 to $30,000 category, over a quarter (28%) fell between $30,000 and $50,000, and another quarter (26%) had a household income of over $50,000.

EXHIBIT 9.4 Survey Report Title Page.

Formatting

Before completing the last section, the table of contents, it's a good idea to check the appearance of the report to make sure that all the formatting is correct, and you may wish to put a finishing touch on the report by inserting headers or footers that print the name of the nonprofit or the name of the report on all the left-hand pages and the title of the current section on the right-hand pages.

Table of Contents

The table of contents will assist the reader who does not have the time to read the whole report to find the detailed discussion on a particular topic that he may be looking for. It should be written only after the rest of the report is complete. Report writers who complete the table of contents before the body of the report is fixed, often find that a later decision to add headers or change other formatting or just to revise a sentence or two can make most or all of the page numbers in the table of contents incorrect.

The table of contents may be as detailed as you wish. For example, readers might find it helpful if not only the sections are numbered but the order in which the individual question results are discussed is displayed, so that the reader can quickly find information on a particular topic.

Conclusion

The information obtained in the research is helpful only to the degree it is communicated to those who can act on it. This chapter suggested guidelines for writing a report whose quality communicates the value of the research.

Conclusion

- Who are my organization's donors and other constituents both demographically and psychographically: that is, what can I learn about their age, gender, race, marital status, children, education, income, and the like, and what can I learn about their lifestyles and values?

- How do my organization's donors and other constituents perceive the organization, both in general and compared to other similar organizations?

- What misperceptions might my organization's donors and other constituents have that could be corrected with the result of improving constituent participation?

- How do my organization's donors and other constituents feel about the communications the organization sends them? What methods—telephone, mail, and so forth—and types of appeals do they like best? What types of communications do they want more of and less of? What topics do they want to hear more about or less about?

- What motivates my organization's donors and other constituents to give and increase their level of giving?

- What causes my organization's donors and other constituents to lapse in their participation?

Your organization can answer all these questions by listening to its donors and other constituents—and not just listening to the ones here and there who take the initiative to talk but listening proactively, scientifically, and accurately to a representative sample of its constituent file.

In the previous chapters, I have discussed how to listen this way to large groups of your donors, members, and clients, that is, how to conduct nonprofit market research. These chapters have looked at both qualitative and quantitative market research. Qualitative research, conducted by means such as focus groups and depth interviews, allows you to delve into the hearts and feelings of a few people. At certain times this is extremely valuable. Nevertheless, it does not generate results that are reliably representative of the larger group you are likely to need to study, that is, your organization's entire donor file.

That is why this book has concentrated on quantitative research and especially surveys, the most prominently used form of quantitative research. To be effective, surveys must ask relevant questions, elicit the specific information the nonprofit seeks, and be conducted among enough people that the answers are reliable from a statistical perspective.

By following the steps outlined in this book, you can

- Identify the primary and supporting objectives for your research.
- Design the type and scope of research that will be best for your organization's mission and budget.
- Devise questions that are effective, objective, and actionable.
- Weave these questions into a questionnaire that is respondent oriented, that encourages the respondent to complete it.
- Analyze the results and organize them into a report.
- Identify additional research techniques that you may wish to use as a nonprofit fundraiser, marketer, and communicator.
- Know what to consider when you are deciding whether to use the services of an outside professional research firm or to do it yourself.

With the advances many organizations in both the for-profit and nonprofit sectors are making in attracting and keeping customers and donors, no nonprofit can afford to stand on the sidelines. Nonprofits' survival requires that they learn to both listen better and appeal better to their donors.

Survey research is one of the techniques that has made a great difference for for-profit organizations. Increasingly, nonprofits of all sizes—small, medium, and large—are also learning to benefit from it. As a result of this research, they are better able to understand their donors and other constituents and communicate messages to them. These nonprofits are motivating people to donate and to participate in other desirable ways. In addition, their donors are more satisfied. They feel their organizations are more responsive to their needs and interests. They are getting the kinds of information they desire, rather than just what organization staff think they might want to hear. And, a very important result, they are giving more.

As you apply the ideas presented here, these results can be yours too.

Resource A: Glossary

Actionable data	Data or results that can easily be implemented or acted upon.
Battery of questions	A series of related questions that use the same set of fixed responses (for example, a scale of 1 to 10 or yes or no).
Bias	An undesirable skew in the survey results that results from giving too much weight to the responses of particular subgroup of the larger population being surveyed.
Biased question	A question that leads the donor to a specific, desired answer (that is, a loaded question).
Bleed effect	The result when the responses or response options for one question affect the responses to or interpretation of a following question.
Blind survey	A survey in which the sponsoring organization is not identified.
BRE	A business reply envelope; a postage-paid, preaddressed envelope included in mail surveys or other communications requesting a response; BREs require a BRE account with the Postal Service.
CATI software	Computer-assisted telephone interviewing software; this software is designed to allow ongoing data entry

during interviews and is usually interactive, facilitating skipping, the rotation of questions and responses, the tracking of sample quotas, and reminding callers of prearranged callback appointments.

Closed-ended questions
Questions that offer respondents a set of all possible responses, and questions that limit responses to preset numbers or preset categories from which the respondent must choose

Cooperation rate
The number of completed interviews divided by the total number of qualified respondents reached. (The total number of qualified respondents reached equals the number of refusals plus the number of completed interviews.)

Cross-tabulation analysis
A breakout of the survey results by various subgroups (for example, by education and income levels, gender, and age).

Demographics
Statistical characteristics of the respondents, such as age, income, and education level.

Depth interviews
One-on-one interviews, usually conducted by telephone, lasting from ten to thirty minutes and generally consisting of open-ended questions. The interviewer follows a discussion guide with each participant and elicits thoughtful, unaided responses.

Estimate of error
The range on either side of a survey percentage result within which the true population percentage is highly likely to occur.

Focus group
A group interview in which a moderator asks participants their feelings and perceptions regarding a certain product, organization, or the like. Similar to a survey; however, group interaction promotes in-depth responses and more insight.

Frequency
How often a particular response to a particular question was chosen, expressed as both a raw number and a percentage.

Incidence	Rate of occurrence, particularly the percentage of names on a list that qualify for the survey.
Interview	A telephone call in which a respondent is asked to complete a questionnaire or an in-person meeting between an interviewer and a respondent.
Interviewer	The person who conducts the call or in-person interview and asks the questions.
Interval scale	A mathematical scale in which each equally sized segment represents the same measurement. Interval scales may be used to segment income, age, number of months since last gift, number of years as a donor or member, size of largest donation, and so forth.
Intrusive questions	Questions that pry too far into the personal lives of the respondents. Among demographic questions, income tends to be perceived as the most intrusive.
Lapsed donor	A donor whose last gift was given so long ago that the organization no longer considers him or her active. Many organizations define lapsed donors as those whose last gift was given twelve or more months ago.
Likert scale	A specific type of scale that usually has a total of five, seven, or nine responses ranging from two extremes (such as *agree* and *disagree*), with the intensity of the response options being symmetrical and with the middle response option indicating neutrality.
Mail surveys	A survey sent through the mail, usually with a cover letter and a business reply envelope.
Major donor	Donors who have given a single or annual gift above a certain amount; the minimum amount that constitutes a major gift is determined by each organization individually.
Monitoring	Listening in on an interview to ensure quality. Some states require that respondents be notified that the calls may be monitored.

Objectives for research	The goals the organization desires to reach as a result of the research.
Open-ended questions	Questions for which the possible responses are not listed for selection but are left entirely up to the espondents. Usually the responses must be categorized later in order to be analyzed.
Ordinal scale	A ranked scale with no objectively measurable distance between the objects or points on the scale (for example, *best, second best, third best*).
Phone surveys	Surveys conducted via the telephone.
Population	The group the nonprofit would like to learn more about. Usually, the survey is conducted among a representative sample of this population.
Prompt	A selection of fixed responses given to the respondent.
Premium	A free item, or gift, included in a mail package to encourage a response.
Pretest questionnaire	A draft questionnaire completed by sample respondents with the goal of improving questionnaire clarity and effectiveness and gauging actual interview time.
Psychographics	The characteristics of respondents' lifestyles, attitudes, perceptions, and feelings (compare *demographics*).
Qualitative research	In-depth research by means such as focus groups, usually done on a small scale and suggestive rather than statistically valid.
Quantitative research	Research designed to obtain answers from enough people (usually a minimum of one hundred) to obtain statistical accuracy.
Range of error	Synonymous with estimate of error: the range on either side of a survey percentage result within which the true population percentage is highly likely to lie.
Recency	How long it has been since a donor gave his or her last gift.
Respondent	The person who answers a questionnaire.

Response rate	The proportion of the people who are offered the questionnaire who actually complete it.
Sample size	The number of completed questionnaires to be obtained in order to estimate the answers of the larger population.
Skipping	Bypassing certain questions as the result of an answer to one or more previous questions. The way skipping occurs in a questionnaire is known as the skip pattern.
Subsample or subgroup	A defined group within the larger group taking a survey (for example, donors among constituents)
Survey software	Software that manages the entry of survey data and the analysis of those data (see also *CATI software*).
Verbal and nonverbal feedback	Verbal feedback is information gained directly from what constituents say (through letters, surveys, focus groups, and so forth), and nonverbal feedback is gained from examining constituents' responses to appeals or other behavioral aspects of their involvement with the organization.
White space	Empty space around printed text, pictures, and graphics that prevents a cluttered look, so the newsletter, appeal, or survey doesn't appear overwhelming to the reader.

Resource B: Exploring Advanced Analyses and What They Can Do for Your Nonprofit

Chapter Eight discussed basic survey analysis. This resource looks at special tools developed in the field of marketing research to take survey information to the next level. These advanced survey analyses are widely used in the for-profit sector, yielding tremendously valuable insights and marketing and communications information. They require experienced statisticians or marketing research analysts as they are driven by advanced statistical procedures such as multiple regression, factor analysis, cluster analysis, CHAID (chi square automatic interaction detector), and discriminant analysis, to name a few.

My purpose is to provide you with a basic sense of what each of the four analyses described here can do for a nonprofit. The following list offers a preview of these analyses:

Qualified Prospect Screening™ enables much greater and more cost-effective fundraising among major donors. It does this by finding the people of wealth who are hidden in the typical donor file and by flagging people on the major donor list who are not currently capable of a major gift. A survey then seeks to reveal what programs or offers will most likely cause each of the best major donor prospects to give and how much to ask for.

Perceptual mapping helps executives learn how constituents and donors view their organization in comparison to competitors and to the donors' ideal organization. This analysis shows organizations which organizational characteristics most differentiate organizations in the minds of the constituents.

Segmentation helps executives understand the different kinds of groups that exist in a donor or constituent file, based on people's values, behaviors, motives, and so forth. It goes beyond direct marketing database segmentation that focuses only on the recency, frequency, and amount of transactions.

Constituent importance modeling moves beyond standard survey results by linking what people say in surveys with what they have actually done (with their giving history, for example). As a result it can show what level of increased giving might result from a given level of change in the donor's perceptions of the organization. This information allows better prioritization of communication efforts and a better sense of how much it would be worth to improve communications.

Major Donor Screening

Your organization may benefit from additional information about its donors. Giving history and contact information are likely not enough data for realizing all the giving of which these donors are capable. Key questions remain:

- Could there be donors on your file who have large incomes or assets and who therefore are capable of making large gifts but of whose potential you are unaware?
- Which of these donors would be receptive to inquiries from your organization regarding major gifts and bequests?

- Which donors have already included your organization in their wills?
- If they haven't already included your organization in their wills, which donors are receptive to doing so?
- Which donors are open to your organization's assistance with planned giving?
- Which of your organization's programs would most motivate each of these major donor prospects?

Among your organization's thousands of donors, there are likely a significant number who have great wealth or income and therefore giving potential. Likewise, many of the donors currently considered major donors may not have any giving potential beyond their current level. A special screening analysis, such as Qualified Prospect Screening™, can prioritize prospecting for both planned and major gifts using data appends, segmentation, and a phone call to assess a prospect's involvement with your organization. Major donor screening might best be conducted as a two-phase process containing the steps outlined in the following sections.

Phase 1: Appending of Wealth Indicators and Initial Prospect Ranking

The first phase involves working with existing donor data and appending new data in the following steps:

1. Donors are ranked according to their historical giving to the organization.
2. Indicators of wealth and income are appended from a number of national databases.
3. Donors are ranked based on their estimated wealth and income.
4. Donors are given an overall score that factors in wealth (from steps 2 and 3) and financial evidence of affinity with the organization (from step 1).

Phase 1 may be done independently of Phase 2, allowing for a good ranking of prospects for major gift and planned giving solicitation. Or it may be combined with Phase 2, allowing for discernment of maximum giving potential.

Phase 2: Telephone Interviews to Maximize Solicitation Success

Letters are sent to the top donors (for example, the top 2,000 found by the composite ranking in step 4 of the first phase) from the president or director of the organization. The letter asks these donors to expect a survey call in the next four weeks because the organization wishes to get to know its donors better and to obtain feedback about the programs and services the donors feel are most important to emphasize at this time.

Next, telephone interviews are conducted with these top prospects. Each call begins with a personal thank-you to the donor for the role he or she has played in the organization's development. As the call continues the caller asks a series of questions to gauge the donor's affiliation, loyalty, and giving potential. The interview results, together with the data appends and giving history information, can be used to derive ratings of each donor's

- Financial ability to make contributions
- Affinity for your organization
- Likelihood of making a planned gift
- Likelihood of making a current major gift

In addition, your organization can determine an overall ranking of all its prospects according to their likelihood of giving a major gift, affinity, and ability to give. It can learn to which program or purpose each donor would be most motivated to give, and it can acquire a better understanding of the maximum the donor might be willing to give, in order that a follow-up call or visit will yield the largest gift possible. Exhibit B.1 presents a prospect profile that illustrates the information that can be obtained for each individual.

Perceptual Mapping: Seeing Through Your Constituents' Eyes

In most survey reports, comparisons are one-dimensional. You look at one chart to learn that donors consider your organization more "responsive" than another. Then you turn the page to find out that you are thought of as less "innovative" than a third of other organizations.

The same thing happens when comparing programs or communication preferences or donor segments. The report of results is thick and impressive, but it's difficult to get a sense of the broad landscape of perceptions.

Perceptual mapping offers an antidote to that difficulty, enabling you to view on a single page the relationships among several different objects across a variety of characteristics. It can confirm your expectations or suggest new areas of opportunity that you might never have been seen otherwise.

When an organization commissions a study, it is hoping to get a grasp on how several different groups see a variety of offerings (or organizations or preferences or behaviors) across a number of dimensions. Yet when we look at data, our brains like to think about only one or two dimensions at a time. Fortunately, computer-based statistical analysis can examine dozens of different dimensions at once, then put data into a format that helps us to see the most important dimensions quickly. That's *perceptual mapping*.

Let's consider a couple of examples. First, let's say an organization wants to examine its image among potential donors. It also wants to see how other, similar organizations are viewed. Survey respondents evaluate the two or three organizations they know best on a variety of characteristics. Then a perceptual map is created from the results, like the one in Figure B.1. This map provides a quick, effective overview of the dimensions on which the organizations are distinguished and shows which organizations are most identified with which attributes.

EXHIBIT B.1 XYZ Wildlife Society Prospect Profile.

PROSPECT SUMMARY

Name:	Lorene Szeim
Birth date:	1948
Number of children:	1
Prospect's feelings about organization:	One of top ten organizations

Qualified prospect ranking (1 = Low, 10 = High):	9
Commitment rating (1 = Low, 10 = High):	10
Total assets (1 = Low, 1,000 = High):	719

CONTACT INFORMATION

Contact name:	Lorene Szeim
Address:	6550 Parkway E
	Harrisburg, PA 17112

Account #:	8397
Spouse's name:	n/a
Telephone:	(717) 652-4560

DEMOGRAPHICS AND LIFESTYLE

Marital status:	Married
Prospect's education level:	College degree
Prospect's employment status:	Full-time
Prospect's occupation:	Homemaker
Estimated household income:	$75,000–$99,999
Homeowner (Yes/No or % Likely):	Yes

Spouse's birth date:	1945
Spouse's education level:	Master's degree
Spouse's employment status:	Full-time
Spouse's occupation:	Oil
Years of residence:	28
Estimated home value:	$354,000

ACTIVITIES

Fraternity or other organizations:	No
Country or private club:	Yes

Membership in	
Church:	Yes
Community service clubs:	No
Leadership in church:	Yes
Leadership in other organizations:	Yes

GIVING HISTORY

First gift date:	5/20/82	Largest gift date:	1/1/93
Lifetime cumulative giving:	$2,095	Largest gift amount:	$450
Lifetime number of gifts:	25	Last gift date:	12/7/99

COMPOSITE SCORES

Affinity (1 = Low, 10 = High):	7	Financial ability (1 = Low, 10 = High):	8
Propensity for current giving (1 = Low, 10 = High):	7	Propensity for planned giving (1 = Low, 10 = High):	9

FINANCIAL DATA

Wealth score (1 = Low, 1,000 = High):	Long-term liquidity (1 = Low, 1,000 = High):	520
760	Short-term liquidity (1 = Low, 1,000 = High):	600
Security assets (1 = Low, 1,000 = High): 600	Financial behavior (Low = 1 [Savers], High = 1,000 [Spenders]:	490

PREFERENCES REGARDING THE WILDLIFE SOCIETY

Animals: *Endangered birds*

Opportunity: *Especially interested in preserving the bald eagle and other N. American birds*

Importance of Additional Projects (1 = Low, 10 = High):

Protecting current wildlife preserves:	3
Declaring additional locations as wildlife preserves:	4
Helping defend specific nearly-extinct creatures:	10
Fighting big business's encroachment into sensitive environments:	6
Educating Americans regarding the importance of protecting wildlife:	9

EXHIBIT B.1 XYZ Wildlife Society Prospect Profile, Cont'd.

AFFINITY FOR XYZ WILDLIFE SOCIETY

(1 = Low, 5 = High)

The quality of the work it performs:	8
The importance of protecting wildlife:	10
The financial integrity of the organization:	6
The leadership of Jim Brown, president of XYZ Wildlife Society:	4

GIVING PREFERENCES

Charities should call donors, present the need, and ask them to donate:	Agree
Charities should prepare for the future by seeking endowments from their donors:	Agree
It is appropriate for a charitable organization to commemorate buildings or parks in honor of donors who make large gifts:	Disagree
Prospect is comfortable with charities presenting specific needs and asking for specific amounts:	Agree

Planned Giving

It is appropriate for a charity to ask donors to consider including the charity in their will:	Yes
What amount or percentage of your assets would you consider appropriate for a bequest?	n/a
Received information about planned giving from XYZ:	Yes
Received information about planned giving from any other organization:	Yes

RESPONDENT RATING

Manner (pleasant, neutral, unpleasant):	Pleasant
Responsiveness (quick to answer, neutral, slow to answer):	Slow to answer
Openness (open, neutral, guarded):	Neutral
Emotional state (emotional, neutral, unemotional):	Emotional

COMMENTS

FIGURE B.1 Sample Perceptual Map.

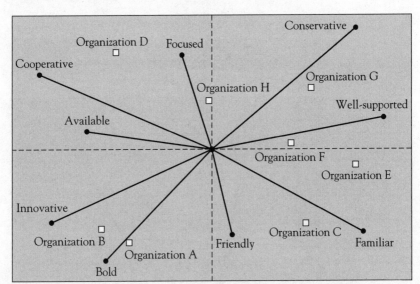

This map is valuable in and of itself. But it becomes even more useful when respondent ideals, preferences, or behaviors are super-imposed on it. For example, in the survey the respondent could have been asked to rate their ideal organization in addition to the existing organizations. The example in Figure B.2 illustrates how a nonprofit TV station's programs were perceived by respondents and also shows respondent preferences, coded by typical viewing/listening times.

In a single graphic, the organization is able to get a feel for

- Some ways current programming is perceived
- Perceived similarities and differences among current programming
- How well viewer preferences are addressed by current programming
- What areas of preference are not adequately addressed by current programs

FIGURE B.2 Sample Perceptual Map with Preferences.

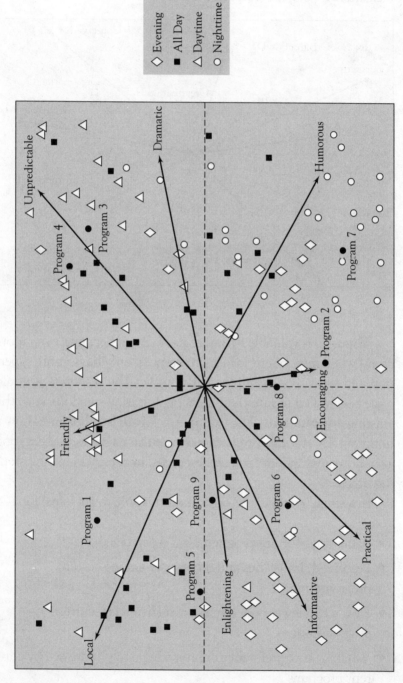

Evening ◇
All Day ■
Daytime △
Nighttime ○

Unpredictable
Dramatic
Humorous
Program 4
Program 3
Program 7
Encouraging ● Program 2
Program 8
Friendly
Program 1
Program 9
Program 6
Program 5
Enlightening
Local
Informative
Practical

- What kinds of programs would work best at various times of day

The same kind of map can be created for giving or purchasing behavior.

Perceptual mapping is a great analysis tool for understanding the public image of an organization, its offerings, and or its competitors. It is particularly helpful for identifying and monitoring positioning strategies.

Segmentation: Valuing Donors' Differences and Similarities

Most nonprofits realize that high-volume donors are valuable enough to justify a one-to-one, customized marketing approach. But for most nonprofits, extending this approach to all donors would require immense resources that cannot be justified by the financial return.

As a result most donors and members receive undifferentiated, mass-produced communications that may or may not match their values and interests. Some organizations segment on the basis of convenient, available information such as recency, frequency, and amount of donor gifts, but rarely do they differentiate based on donor interests and values.

Segmentation provides a middle ground in marketing. It allows an organization to target marketing communications toward individual preferences without overburdening scarce resources. A segmentation approach recognizes that the same product or service can appeal to different people for different reasons. Although segmentation acknowledges individual differences, it also recognizes that many people have very similar values, needs, and preferences. Therefore, segmentation identifies groups of similar people. This allows nonprofits to deliver targeted messages to a handful of groups rather than a large number of individuals.

> Segmentation Joke 1: There are two types of people in the world: those who divide people into groups, and those who don't.

Segmentation works especially well under certain market conditions:

Condition 1: segments actually exist. Donors and prospects really have differing values or behaviors, nevertheless many people share each value or behavior or sets of values or behaviors.

Condition 2: segments are identifiable. Your organization can obtain information from individual donors or members about their behavior, values, or motivations.

Condition 3: segments can be reached through targeted messages. It is possible to communicate with donors and members through means other than the mass media (for example, direct advertising, personal sales, customer service contacts, or even billing).

Condition 4: constituents' values and behavior are relatively stable. The segments your organization defines aren't going to be out of date next week.

Membership organizations, direct marketers, and many other organizations typically meet these conditions very well.

> Segmentation Joke 2: There are three types of people in the world: those who can count and those who can't.

Once you have decided to use segmentation, the key issue is determining how your organization will define the groups. Many organizations use demographic variables to create segments—gender, for example. This is a convenient way to group people, but it is not often the most strategic—unless most women give or join for one reason and most men do so for another.

Behavioral measures are better than demographic ones because they let donors group themselves. For example, many organizations use one marketing strategy for frequent or loyal donors and another for infrequent or lapsed donors. But when behavior is a reflection of values and attitudes, a more strategic method is to group donors or members based on the values their decisions reflect or the needs they seek to fill. This enables the nonprofit to craft communications based directly on the values, needs and preferences of those it seeks to reach and motivate. The likely result will be communications that receive greater attention and a better response. Moreover, this approach will encourage loyalty to the cause or organization that is in touch with its donors and their needs.

The first step in performing this kind of segmentation is to survey a sample of donors or prospects or both, including in the survey a list of statements about attitudes, values, needs, or behavior and asking participants to rate their personal level of agreement or disagreement with each statement.

The researcher then uses cluster analysis to define segments on the basis of response patterns. This process allows the people responding to define the number and character of their own segments. It examines data for both similarities and differences, using them to group constituents who are most similar to one another and most different from others. Using other variables from the survey or constituent database, the segments are then described in detail.

Next, the survey results are used to help identify the segment of each person in the database (not just those surveyed). There are two options for doing this. First, a statistical scoring model can be created based on database variables only. The more complete and detailed the database, the more accurate the model. The model will include a measure of accuracy. In many cases, however, the database variables alone will not be sufficient to score donors and prospects with a high degree of accuracy. In these cases, another model can be used to identify the key questions that best predict segment membership. These few questions can be asked of all current donors or members through a quick mail or phone survey. Most people are willing to share their needs and preferences with those who are interested in serving them better and being more responsive to their needs. A similar brief survey form may be distributed as part of a welcome mailing to new donors and members in order to keep the database current.

Once the database is scored and every constituent has been assigned to a segment, targeted communications can commence!

Constituent Importance Modeling

What's *really* important to your constituents? Just how important is it? And what should you do about it?

The answers to questions like these can be discovered in importance modeling. Importance modeling doesn't just tell you what people think is important, it also reveals how their attitudes influence their giving.

And the Importance Model doesn't stop there. Using multivariate statistical modeling, it also shows you the potential value (in dollars and cents) of improving constituent attitudes, helping you to plan your organization's communication efforts.

To see the value of creating an Importance Model, let's contrast the ABC Nonprofit, which does not use importance modeling, with the XYZ Nonprofit, which does use importance modeling.

The ABC Nonprofit asks its donors how the organization is perceived in terms of such characteristics as these:

- Providing a unique service
- Remaining focused on its mission
- Spending donors' money wisely
- Demonstrating how lives are changed

It also asks how important each objective is to the donors.

ABC gets traditional results based on descriptive statistics and cross-tabulations. Although all the objectives are considered relatively important by the respondents, two are rated significantly less important than the others. ABC's leaders also find out that the organization is perceived as strong in certain areas and as somewhat weaker in others. Major donors are observed to give significantly higher ratings than other donors on nearly every objective.

ABC's leaders conclude that the more people like the organization, the more they tend to give (and vice versa). Therefore, they decide the organization should continue to use informative communication to foster goodwill and persuasive communication to encourage giving. Both types of communication, they decide, should emphasize objectives that are considered important.

The XYZ Nonprofit asks its donors the same questions, but it gets expanded results based on statistical modeling. First, the importance of attitudes is considered—both as stated by donors and as calculated in terms of *their impact on giving.* The model uses statistical techniques to quantify the association between attitudes and giving, so the organization does not have to rely solely on stated importance ratings. A chart such as the one in Figure B.3 compares the two dimensions and notes the implications for donor communications. Consider the top four attributes shown on this chart. The organizational attribute of changed lives, although only a slight favorite in terms of stated importance, is the dominant attribute in terms of influencing giving. Spending wisely scores high for both stated and derived importance. Being mission focused is said to be important by respondents but has a relatively minor impact on giving. Meanwhile, providing a unique service affects giving much more strongly than its stated importance would indicate.

The implications XYZ's leaders draw are that the organization should

- Make sure every communications piece makes reference to how lives are changed.
- Seek opportunities to report news about how well money is spent.

FIGURE B.3 Stated Importance of Attributes Versus Actual Influence on Giving.

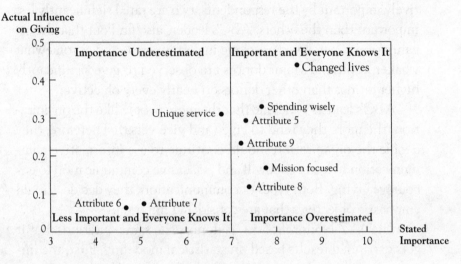

- Emphasize the uniqueness of the organization, particularly near the conclusion of appeals.

- Not deemphasize staying mission focused yet not be overly concerned about the implications of taking on new kinds of projects.

In addition to explaining existing giving behavior, statistical models are also useful for predicting giving behavior. Changes in attitude are likely to affect giving, and a model can help your organization simulate the impact of attitude shifts on gift income. Table B.1 shows how XYZ Nonprofit was able to use the Importance Model to explore what improvements in respondents' ratings of the organization's attributes might mean in terms of giving. For each attribute tested the table displays the current average performance rating from respondents, a measure of the ease of improving the rating (based on the consistency of each rating and room for improvement), a target mean (based on the ease of improvement), and an estimate of the dollar impact of achieving the goal.

TABLE B.1 Possible Impact of Ratings Improvement.

Organizational Attribute	Current Mean	Ease of Improving	Target Mean	Dollar Impact of Reaching Target (Annual)
Providing a unique service	5.3	High	6.3	$86,483
(Attribute 5)	7.3	Medium	7.8	40,452
Demonstrating how lives are changed	8.8	Low	9.0	24,550
Remaining focused on its mission	7.0	Medium	7.5	23,713
(Attribute 9)	8.3	Low	8.6	19,249
Spending donors' money wisely	8.5	Low	8.7	18,413
(Attribute 6)	5.8	High	6.8	16,739
(Attribute 8)	8.3	Low	8.6	10,043
(Attribute 7)	6.9	Low	7.2	5,859

The XYZ Nonprofit used the dollar projections in the table to help it establish communication priorities. Because the ratings for providing a unique service are both important and changeable, efforts directed at improving constituents' perceptions of uniqueness are likely to be rewarded. In fact, such efforts are likely to be more than twice as beneficial as similar efforts on behalf of other perceptions. Other attributes are either not easily changed (as is the case for spending donors' money wisely), not important (as for Attribute 6), or a combination of both (as for Attribute 7). (Note, however, that for several reasons, figures from this kind of analysis are not to be used as financial projections for budgeting purposes. The purpose of the analysis is not to predict actual giving increases but to prioritize communications issues.)

In the end, although both organizations collected the same data, the XYZ Nonprofit came away with much more useful and actionable information. And because data collection accounts for the greatest proportion of research expense, XYZ's research investment was only marginally more than ABC's.

Consider how an Importance Model might help your organization not only to quantify what is important to its donors but also to quantify the value of its efforts on their behalf.

Each of the four advanced analyses reviewed here involves survey data but produces meaningful results that go well beyond what can be obtained by simply looking at a survey's percentage results.

Resource C: When and How to Use a Professional Researcher

Whether to make or to buy; that is the question! There is a lot more to good surveying than meets the eye, and thus there are many advantages to hiring a research firm. These firms often produce the best results. However, sometimes the research can be conducted more cost effectively in house. This resource outlines the many aspects to consider when trying to reach a make or buy decision. It also discusses how to select the best research provider if your nonprofit elects to work with one and what to expect during that working relationship.

First, let's review the advantages of each approach: conducting research in house versus conducting it with an outside researcher.

Advantages of Conducting the Research In-House

The advantages of conducting a survey in-house are relatively intuitive, and they mostly center around saving money. Here are a few examples of circumstances that would support a nonprofit in a decision to conduct constituent research in house:

- The nonprofit has a full-time researcher on staff, and the executives who will use the research results are confident of the researcher's objectivity.

- A volunteer who is a professional researcher offers to help. Occasionally, a board member or a volunteer who is a professional survey researcher will offer to help the nonprofit either free of charge or at an exceptionally low price. If the nonprofit is to receive all the researcher's services free of charge, this might outweigh the advantages of going with a researcher who specializes in research for nonprofits.

- The nonprofit's budget is so constrained that if the nonprofit does not do the research in house, it will not do it at all.

Of course, the latter reason is the one that most frequently causes nonprofit executives to conduct their research in house. If your organization falls in this category, take heart. The information in the preceding chapters will help you to help your organization conduct a much more accurate and effective survey than would likely be possible otherwise.

Advantages of Hiring a Professional Research Firm

There are a number of advantages to working with an outside expert.

- *Experience*. The staff of a research firm usually have decades of collective experience in conducting surveys. Specifically, they will know whether, how much, and in what form both qualitative and quantitative research will be helpful. They will likely be able to suggest which subgroup(s) to include and which sample sizes will be most appropriate.

- *Proven questions*. If you select a provider that specializes in nonprofit organizations, the staff likely will have a large collection of survey questions they have developed, tested, and refined. Frequently, these will be questions that other nonprofits have found to provide actionable insights and to lead to good decision making.

- *Comparisons with other nonprofits.* When reading the results of a survey, it is very helpful to know whether the results are good, bad, or indifferent compared with the survey results of other similar organizations. For example, if the average income of a nonprofit's donors is $35,000, how does that compare with donor income nationally or with incomes among the general U.S. population? If 50 percent of a nonprofit's donors say they *feel well informed,* 35 percent say they *feel somewhat informed,* and 15 percent say they *do not feel well informed,* are these results better than those most nonprofits would obtain, or are they perhaps worse? Should an executive reading these results be troubled and redevelop her donor education program, or should she be elated and work on higher priorities? Research firms that have been specializing in nonprofits may have been compiling their results and may be able to compare the findings for your organization with accumulated results for a large number of other nonprofits, giving you better decision-making ability.

- *Experienced fielding.* Professional research firms are likely to have good survey fielding services. Their telephone interviewers are likely to be experienced and trained in proper research techniques. Their survey researchers are likely to be experienced not just in general research but in researching donor populations. Even in the task of efficiently and accurately compiling a mailing, the research firm may have more experience than a nonprofit and may therefore achieve more accurate results.

- *Objectivity.* It is easy for those new to survey research to unconsciously word questions in ways that bias people's answers. It is especially easy when the person is personally involved with the nonprofit and has a vested interest in the nonprofit's success.

- *Credibility.* In our nearly two decades of nonprofit research and interviewing experience, my colleagues and I have noticed that studies conducted by professional research firms carry a lot more weight with decision makers. Board members and senior managers seem more impressed and much more likely to act on the results than to read them and file them away. They may be influenced by the firm's experience or by the *halo effect* that suggests that outsiders can do a better job. Another reason for their attitude may be that when people pay more money for something, they are more likely to value the results. For whatever reason, studies by professional firms tend to be viewed with greater credibility and to be acted on with more confidence.

- *Efficiency and possibly lower costs*. Because a professional research firm is likely to have greater experience than the nonprofit, it is also likely that this firm can conduct survey research more efficiently. Given this efficiency, it is very likely that the firm's service will cost less overall than performing the research internally. This is especially true when the nonprofit also considers the opportunity costs of the work that its staff forego when conducting survey work and the overhead costs associated with these staff.

If you think you may benefit from employing a professional research firm, the next section of this resource will help you maximize the value of your research dollar.

What to Look for When Choosing a Research Vendor

It is helpful to keep several things in mind when looking for a research vendor. Here are a few of the most important items.

First, when obtaining multiple bids, make sure you are making apples-to-apples comparisons. Buying research is different from buying most tangible commodities. Often, when a nonprofit requests bids for constituent research, it specifies the kinds of information it is seeking or what it wants to be able to do as a result of the information and asks the research firm to suggest an appropriate study design. When this is the case, simply matching two or more firms' prices is an insufficient comparison. Rarely do two firms recommend the same research design, so it is also necessary to compare exactly what kind of research one is getting for the cost quoted. When one firm's proposal looks much stronger in terms of the firm's relevant experience, understanding of your needs, or creativity in the research design, it may be best to choose that firm to ensure getting the quality you need. If the price is higher than your nonprofit's financial capability, simply ask for a redesign that fits your available budget. If two prospective vendors seem to offer the same quality of services, but their research designs differ a little, you might pick the design that you feel is best, and then request that the firms rebid based on that design. In this case it is best to specify as many of the survey features as possible so that the bids will represent a fair comparison.

Here are some survey features you might specify when asking for bids:

- The number of questionnaires
- The length of the questionnaire
- The number of subgroups to be sampled
- Whether or not an on-site presentation of results is desired
- The incidence of the list to be called. *Incidence* in this context refers to the percentage of names on the list or database that you will be using that will qualify for the survey. For example, if a survey of all donors is to be conducted and everyone on the list is a donor, then the incidence will be 100 percent. However, if you are planning a prospect survey and only those who answer the first few questions a certain way will qualify as prospects, then the incidence may vary greatly, as will the price of conducting the research owing to the greater number of calls to be made or surveys to be mailed.

- The expected response rate. Even when the incidence rate for your list is very high or even 100 percent, the response rate will be lower, and it will vary depending on other characteristics of the population surveyed. For example, if a survey is of donors and it is not conducted blind, the response rate may be 80 percent to 90 percent, but if a survey is blind and it is conducted among lapsed donors, the response rate may be only 50 percent. Such factors will have significant implications for the cost of the research.

- The number of open-ended questions desired.

- The extent of the statistical analysis required.

- Whether the nonprofit will provide the list of names and phone numbers or whether the research firm will be expected to acquire or compile an appropriate list.

Second, look for someone with a great deal of experience in researching on behalf of nonprofits and, if possible, someone experienced in working with a nonprofit similar to your own.

Third, do not be overly concerned by the location of the researcher. In this day of advanced technology, geography is much less critical than it used to be. It is almost always better to deal with someone experienced in meeting nonprofit needs, even if it means communicating mostly by phone, fax, e-mail, Express Mail, and the like, than it is to work with a researcher who is nearby but who has less experience with the nonprofit realm.

Finally, consider each firm's client list. Does the research firm have reputable clients? Does the firm have clients similar to your organization?

Attending to these guidelines will help you identify a good research vendor. Another suggestion is to contact organizations similar to yours to ask whom they would recommend and why.

Once you have selected a professional research firm, it is a good idea to put your agreement with that firm in writing, including the research features specified, to avoid later misunderstandings. The agreement may also specify how payment for the work is to be handled. Typically, payment is made in portions throughout a project, perhaps one-third on project approval, one-third during the fieldwork, and the last third on completion of the final report. In Chapter Two you can find a full overview of how the research progresses with either an in-house or external researcher.

Resource D: The Nonprofit Researcher's Toolkit

In this book I have focused almost exclusively on what I believe is the most useful tool for listening to your donors—survey research. There are, however, quite a number of other research techniques that are valuable in specific situations. This resource sketches those that should be part of any nonprofit researcher's thinking about how to listen to donors.

Qualitative Research Techniques

In Chapter Two I defined several types of research including qualitative research, mentioning that qualitative research does not seek to provide quantifiable results as surveys do. Instead, it seeks to reveal those types of information that do not lend themselves to quantification, such as people's feelings and emotions and the kinds of thoughts that surface in creative or brainstorming sessions. Two methods of qualitative research that can be particularly informative for nonprofits are the focus group and the one-on-one interview.

The Focus Group

A focus group is basically a group interview. It is like a survey, but the participants are interviewed in person, face to face, and asked to share in much greater depth. They also hear each other's responses and interact with one another, which in turn, stimulates more discussion on the issues being investigated. The typical focus group session lasts for two hours, is led by a professional research moderator, and includes six to twelve participants.

Focus groups are similar to surveys in that both methods allow the organization to ask questions of a targeted population. The difference is that surveys must focus on more superficial questions, those that don't require much thinking on the part of the respondents. The answers are usually limited to yes or no or multiple-choice lists. The respondents do not usually have much time to spare and therefore won't provide extensive answers even if prompted. However, surveys can be conducted with many people and the results summarized by percentages that fairly accurately reflect the relative opinions of larger populations (for example, 30 percent said *yes*, 65 percent said *no*, and 5 percent were *not sure*). For this reason surveys are considered quantitative research.

Focus groups are considered qualitative research because they provide a look at the quality of the deeper feelings of the participants. As these donors discuss the issues of interest to the nonprofit, they become increasingly in touch with their feelings and share them candidly. The moderator can be spontaneous, not scripted, probing further when important topics are raised. Focus groups are excellent for gaining insights useful for a variety of nonprofit purposes, such as these:

- Evaluation and improvement of a current fundraising program or campaign
- Design of a proposed fundraising program or campaign
- Evaluation and improvement of a newsletter or magazine
- Evaluation and improvement of such communication efforts as brochures, direct-mail packages, telethons, and TV and radio spots
- Evaluation of the potential for success in targeting a new market or niche

A focus group permits a discussion of the issues an organization is concerned about by the constituents themselves. It is best moderated by a neutral third party who is experienced in this type of research. After the issues and target audience have been identified, the organization's researcher, who may be the same person as the moderator, drafts a *screener* and a *discussion guide*. The screener is a short survey that incorporates an invitation to participate in the focus group and that is used by telephone recruiters. It accomplishes two purposes. First, it screens out all the people on the calling list who do not have the particular characteristics desired by the researcher (for example, for a particular focus group the organization might not be interested in those under thirty-five, those who do not qualify as donor prospects, and the like). Second, it allows the researcher to learn more about those who are recruited, particularly with regard to issues relevant to the forthcoming discussion.

The discussion guide is a carefully prepared list of perhaps a dozen or so questions that the moderator will ask the group. The questions are not necessarily read verbatim. Each is open-ended and allows for as many spontaneous subquestions as the moderator feels will be helpful.

When the nonprofit is using a professional research firm, both the screener and discussion guide are submitted to the nonprofit for suggestions and eventual approval. Once the screener is approved, the recruiting begins. The list of names usually comes from the organization or it may be rented. Each recruit is invited to a discussion group at a specific time and place. Focus groups are usually held on weekday nights at 6 P.M. or 8 P.M., when most people are available. Recruits are usually offered a cash incentive ranging from $25 to $50 per person. The 6 P.M. participants are also usually served a deli dinner.

The location may depend on the needs of the client organization; however, focus groups are usually best conducted in professional facilities designed specifically for this purpose. They feature a well-appointed discussion room with a large oval table and a one-way minor. The organization's staff view the discussion through the one-way mirror from an adjacent room. The focus group room has hidden or unobtrusive microphones and a video camera.

Before starting, the moderator always mentions that he has some associates behind the mirror and that the discussion is being recorded. Usually, the name of the sponsoring organization is not revealed so as to reduce bias in the participants' responses as much as possible.

The first question is usually aimed at breaking the ice and developing some group cohesiveness. This is followed by some general questions, such as, What do you think of the X type of not-for-profits? These general questions are designed to be nonintrusive and easy to answer so that the participants become comfortable with the discussion and begin thinking about the issues at hand. The questions at the core of the nonprofit's concerns are usually saved for the end of the focus group. By this time the participants are more relaxed and are sharing very candidly. Because the earlier questions were general, the participants may not yet have surmised the name of the sponsoring organization.

At least once during the group interview, usually toward the end, the moderator will give the group a short task to work on and excuse himself from the room for a few minutes. During this time he ducks into the observation room to see if the discussion has raised any further questions the observers might like to ask.

After the focus group is concluded, the participants are thanked and paid the promised fee. The moderator and the observers then usually discuss the insights they gained from the focus group.

Focus group research may involve anywhere from one group (for a limited study) to eight groups or more (for very large studies). Two, four, or six groups are most commonly used. Listening to additional groups gives a nonprofit a better chance of learning which are truly the most common feelings and issues among participants and of avoiding the skewed perceptions that might result from a single group that chanced to have an unusual mix of participants. In order to obtain a representative cross-section of participants, the groups may also be held in varied geographical locations (for example, in New York, Chicago, and Los Angeles, for a national organization), they may differ demographically (centering on either African Americans or Caucasians, for example, on either older donors or younger donors, or on either prospects or donors), or they may differ in some other relevant way.

After the entire series of focus groups is complete, the researcher usually systematically reviews and analyzes all the interviews and produces a written report and sometimes a live presentation of the results as well. The audiotapes and videotapes are also available to the nonprofit.

Focus groups are a tried and true methodology that can improve constituent satisfaction and have a direct and positive impact on income. They have been used with great effect by the for-profit sector and can benefit nonprofits as well.

One-on-One Depth interviews

One-on-one depth interviews are essentially the same as focus groups in their purpose and in the questions asked, however, as the name implies, they are conducted with single individuals rather than groups. They may be conducted either in person or on the telephone. Focus groups seem to be more popular than these individual interviews, but there are still occasions when one-on-one interviews are preferred. Here is a comparison of the advantages of each method.

Advantages of Focus Groups

- They can be viewed as they occur.
- The interaction between constituents produces more results.
- Focus groups are easy to video- and audiotape.
- They are conducive to exhibits (e.g., video, appeals, newsletters).

Advantages of One-on-One Interviews

- The effects of peer pressure are reduced.

- They can be conducted by phone in locales where there are few constituents.

- They are less expensive if conducted by phone.

Two Traditional Nonprofit Research Studies

Two studies that may be of particular value to nonprofits are the feasibility study and prospect research.

The Feasibility Study

A feasibility study is often conducted prior to a capital, endowment, or special project campaign to learn whether there is sufficient interest to sustain a successful campaign and to determine how the campaign should be designed. This study involves talking one on one with some of the major constituents of the organization, such as members of the board of directors, major benefactors, alumni, and the like. It may also include a mail or phone survey or focus groups directed to midlevel donors. As a result of this preliminary research, the organization will have a better idea of how high to set the campaign's philanthropic goal, what organization needs will best motivate the constituents to give during the campaign, what messages or themes will generate the most interest, and who needs to be involved. This research also has an important function beyond any information it gathers; it should sow the seed among the major prospective donors so that when fundraising begins these people are already aware of the campaign, feel involved, and are motivated to participate.

Prospect Research

Prospect research involves obtaining information about individuals, corporations, or foundations thought to have an interest in donating to the organization; its purpose is to increase the likelihood of receiving large gifts. A perfect example of how such research might come about occurs when an organization looks at its donor or prospect list and realizes that it is likely to contain many people who have exceptionally large incomes or wealth and who could give a lot if they were asked and motivated to give. The organization therefore seeks to find out who these people are by networking or using public records of such indicators as auto, boat, or airplane ownership; home ownership; home sale price; insider stock transactions; buying habits; lifestyle data; and so on. Much of this information can be obtained by purchasing demographic overlays for the nonprofit's database from organizations that compile national databases of this information.

A good way of following up once names have been identified is to conduct a survey to determine which of these current donors or prospects are the most likely to donate more or to begin donating and how to best approach them. Specifically, the nonprofit might seek to learn how the prospect feels about the nonprofit, what the individual's strongest motivations for giving might be, and what level of gift might be successfully solicited. Asking questions about the prospect's family or other interests may be helpful in order to better connect with him or her.

Data Analysis Techniques for Nonprofit Direct Marketers

This section offers a few additional ways to analyze data about donors and other constituents in order to improve the cost effectiveness of appeals and acquisition efforts.

Improve Direct-Mail Testing with Factorial Analysis

Direct-mail professionals continually seek opportunities to develop more effective mailings. Factorial analysis is a statistical tool that allows direct mailers to quickly and effectively test hundreds of combinations of package elements to learn which ones perform best. This method allows mailers to roll out to a wide audience with more confidence.

Those who design direct-mail packages frequently test new design elements to see what works, using different combinations of offer, envelope size, teaser copy, ask strategy, and letter length. Sometimes many different packages are tested to find the best ones. Of course, there may be literally thousands of possible combinations of the various design elements you might choose from. For example, if you were planning a direct-mail package and were faced with decisions regarding

- Two types of teaser copy
- Two letter lengths
- Two motivational offers
- Two ask strategies
- Three graphic design themes
- Two envelope sizes

you would have ninety-six possible combinations to choose from!

You might consider testing several different combinations—but never all ninety-six! However, factorial analysis provides a statistical design that considers all ninety-six possible combinations based on the results of just eight test packages. The analysis creates test packages, or profiles, that combine the various design elements in such a way that the impact of each element can be measured independently of the others.

This technique also works for smaller test designs. For example, testing four things with two factors each can give you readings on 16 different combinations. Similarly, testing nine things with two factors each can help you assess 256 possible combinations.

Here's how a factorial-based test would work for the example given earlier with ninety-six possible combinations:

1. Identify the various design elements you want to test and the alternatives being considered for each element. Feed those elements into a statistical program that can generate a factorial

design for, in this case, eight different combinations of the elements. This will require advanced software such as SPSS or SAS.

2. Produce and mail the eight test packages to a sample audience of five thousand or more. The profile for this sample audience must be the same for each package you mail, so that no package will outperform or underperform another because of the characteristics of the sample audience rather than the characteristics of the package.

3. Capture two kinds of response data: (1) the number of responses and (2) the average gift or purchase size. These response results are fed into a factorial analysis program, which then calculates the relative value of each design element.

4. Design a package with the optimal combination of elements (most likely this optimal package will *not* be exactly the same as any of the original eight test packages), retest, and roll out to generate much more response and income!

Factorial modeling not only identifies the optimal combination of elements but can also predict just how that package (or any other) is likely to perform. Therefore, the value of the analysis can be clearly calculated by comparing the predicted results from the optimal package to the results from a control package (that is, the one most closely resembling past mailings) or management's best guess.

Figure D.1 presents an example of a spreadsheet-based model that displays this comparison.

Another benefit of factorial analysis is that compared to traditional panel testing it provides greater confidence in the results. Recall that eight packages were suggested by the factorial analysis software in the first step of the example. Each of those eight packages features a combination of design elements, not just one element (as it would in traditional analysis). Therefore the audience that sees element one through element eight effectively increases by two, three, or even five or six times (depending on how many elements are being tested). With more eyeballs comes more confidence in the results.

FIGURE D.1 Sample Results of a Factorial-Based Comparison.

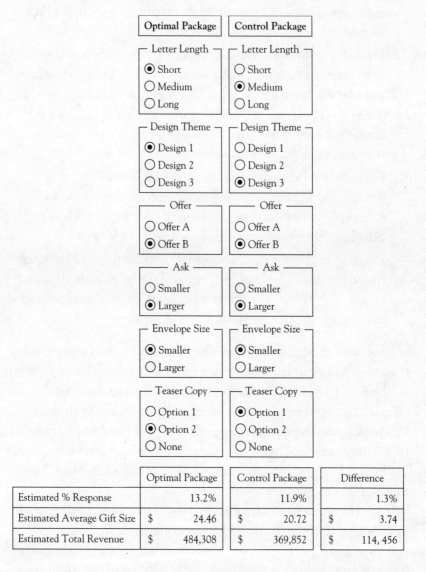

	Optimal Package	Control Package	Difference
Estimated % Response	13.2%	11.9%	1.3%
Estimated Average Gift Size	$ 24.46	$ 20.72	$ 3.74
Estimated Total Revenue	$ 484,308	$ 369,852	$ 114,456

Also, because more of the target audience sees each element you test, you can retest and have the confidence to roll out to wider audiences than you would attempt after traditional testing. This means that you can reach more people faster with the best strategies—and have more confidence in the results, too!

Of course, your organization can and should compare actual retest and rollout results to the results predicted by the factorial design model. And of course using this method does not prevent an organization from testing totally new creative concepts outside the factorial analysis matrix.

Lifetime Donor Value: A Powerful Analysis Technique[1]

For years nonprofits have been evaluating their donor acquisition efforts based on percentage response, average gift, and other short-term statistical results. As a result, many nonprofits have suffered in the long run, raising far fewer funds than they could have. Increasingly, nonprofits are tracking the actual long-term value to date of their donors. They then compare these long-term values to the long-term cost to date of the same donors. The long-term cost includes the cost of maintaining the average donor and cultivating his value, as well as the cost of acquisition. Some organizations then go to the next step and project these long-term values and costs to lifetime values (LTVs) and lifetime costs (LTCs).

What are the benefits of lifetime value analysis? Many! Tracking LTVs and LTCs will allow you to identify the

- Best donor acquisition sources (direct mail, space ads, events, telemarketing, TV, and so forth)
- Most profitable subsources (particular lists, periodicals, events, radio stations, geomarkets [geographically defined markets], and the like)
- Best offers (which donor motivations to appeal to, for example)
- Best asks (whether to ask for a low or high dollar amount, a single gift or a pledge, for example)

Lifetime value analysis can also help you learn

[1] This discussion of lifetime donor value, including Figures D.2 and D.3, and Tables D.1 and D.2, is adapted from B. Campbell, "Lifetime Donor Value," *Fund Raising Management,* July 1994, pp. 16–18. Reprinted with permission.

- What the maximum is you can spend to acquire a donor and still hit your income-to-cost target
- Whether your acquisition program is becoming more or less healthy over time
- What the fundraising overhead ratio (lifetime income divided by lifetime cost) is for each effort

Using LTV to Focus Donor Acquisition. One nonprofit, I'll call it the ABC Nonprofit, that conducted lifetime value analysis found that the LTV of its donors acquired from different sources varied widely, from $133 to more than $2,000. (This organization has unusually high lifetime values. The typical nonprofit's LTVs vary from $50 to $500.) These results are displayed in Figure D.2.

With the help of an analyst, the organization then estimated the lifetime costs. The LTVs were divided by the LTCs, producing lifetime value–lifetime cost ratios. These ratios are displayed in Figure D.3.

Notice the wide spread in the ratios in Figure D.3, from 1.8 to 8.2. What a tremendous help this information was to the organization. Right away the executives knew where to focus the organi-

FIGURE D.2 ABC Nonprofit's Lifetime Donor Values by Source.

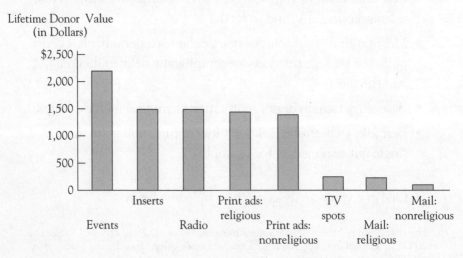

Lifetime Donor Value
(in Dollars)

zation's acquisition budget. They spent it on the sources generating the highest ratios.

Prior to looking at lifetime value, this organization had looked only at short-term results. Consider what would have happened if it had continued to allocate its acquisition budget based only on acquisition cost per new donor, as displayed in Table D.1.

FIGURE D.3 ABC Nonprofit's Lifetime Value–Lifetime Cost Ratios by Source.

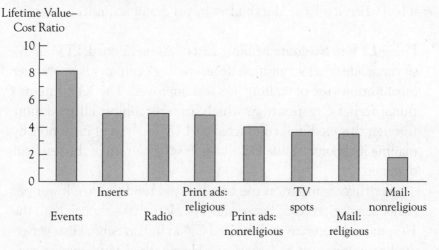

TABLE D.1 ABC Nonprofit's Evaluation of Donor Sources Using Lifetime Value.

Donor Source	Lifetime Value	Lifetime Cost	Lifetime Value: Lifetime Cost	Acquisition Cost per New Donor
Events	$1,430	$175	8.2	$52
Inserts	1,460	284	5.1	128
Radio	2,125	415	5.1	193
Print ads: religious	1,458	305	4.8	145
Print ads: nonreligious	1,364	346	3.9	183
TV spots	373	129	2.9	73
Mail: religious	322	124	2.6	68
Mail: nonreligious	133	72	1.8	49

Table D.1 is ordered by lifetime value-to-cost ratios and also displays the acquisition cost per new name. Notice how many of the sources with the lowest donor acquisition costs also had relatively low lifetime value-cost ratios. Prior to this analysis, these sources would likely have been the ones organization executives preferred. They would have avoided the sources with the highest donor acquisition costs, even though these were the most profitable in the long run. Once this nonprofit allocated its acquisition budget according to lifetime income-cost ratios, it generated about twice the income it had when it allocated its budget by per donor acquisition cost.

Using LTV to Evaluate Mailing Lists. As mentioned, LTV analysis can guide other acquisition decisions. Let's consider how another organization's use of mailing lists was improved. The XYZ International Relief Organization, which acquires almost all its donors through this medium, conducted an LTV analysis of its donors by mailing list source. Table D.2 illustrates the pattern of the results it obtained.

For this organization the best lists did tend to have lower per donor acquisition costs, but not always. Note that although both the Hospitalized Veterans and the Red Cloud Indian School lists generated new donors at $14 each, the Hospitalized Veterans list generated almost $6 of income for every dollar of cost, whereas the other list barely paid for itself over the entire life of the donors acquired from it! Also, the Cancer Research Fund list had a per donor acquisition cost ($18) very close to that of the National M.S. list ($15). However, the latter generated more than three times the value, with a value-cost ratio twice that of the former.

Needless to say, this organization was very glad it had looked at the lifetime value of its mailing list acquired donors.

How to Project Lifetime Values. To obtain lifetime projections, donors' giving is usually projected out to as long as ten years. Because income received several years from today is worth less than income received today, the income of future years is discounted

TABLE D.2 XYZ Organization's Lifetime Value–Lifetime Cost Ratios.

Mailing List	Acquisition Cost	Lifetime Costs	Lifetime Value	Lifetime Value: Lifetime Cost	Number of Donors
Children International	$4	$18	$108	6.1	256
Little Brothers/Sisters	6	22	127	5.7	133
Hospitalized Vets	14	35	186	5.4	148
CARE	12	31	167	5.3	1,301
National M.S. Society	15	37	195	5.3	474
Donors to Fight Cancer	24	35	90	2.6	266
Cancer Research Fund	18	26	64	2.4	268
Cystic Fibrosis	25	36	77	2.1	707
Red Cloud Indian School	14	20	23	1.1	109

using the *present value* method. This is widely used in the financial industry to project the value of many things including all types of loans, investments, and the like.

Technical Considerations. Special care needs to be taken to avoid overestimating lifetime values due to unusually large gifts. However, these gifts should not be removed from consideration altogether, and the donor source should receive credit for generating them. Statistical techniques are available for reducing the *noise* caused by such gifts.

Donor or Customer File Audit

The donor performance analysis (DPA) is also known as a file audit. This analysis of a database pinpoints strengths and weaknesses in a nonprofit's funding patterns. The key indicators can be tracked to learn how new, continuing, multi-year, and lapsed constituents are trending. The result is often a forty-plus-page report that identifies trends in the donor or member file in response rates, annual cumulative giving, average gift size, frequency of giving, attrition rates, and more. The statistical analysis is ideally followed by an action-oriented written analysis, graphs, and tables that help executives and staff visualize the key information and that point out possible areas for improvement. Executives can identify the actionable intelligence that holds the greatest potential for improving the organization's funding. Table D.3 illustrates some findings from a donor performance analysis.

Segmentation Analysis

Many nonprofits that rely on direct marketing to acquire and maintain donors have large donor files. They know that it is cost effective to segment these files into a variety of homogeneous groups with respect to their giving potential, such as small donors, middle donors, large donors, recent donors and less recent donors, frequent

TABLE D.3 Fundraising Overview Report.

Donor Status Beginning of Year	1996	1997	1998	1999	% Change '96–'99
	New Donors (First Gift This Year)				
Number Acquired This Year	2,731	1,916	2,095	2,221	–19%
Number of Gifts	3,873	2,963	3,103	3,725	–4%
Value of Gifts	$338,190	$305,127	$281,326	$366,047	8%
Avg. # of Gifts/Donor	1.4	1.5	1.5	1.7	18%
Average Gift Size	$87	$103	$91	$98	13%
Annual Giving/Donor	$124	$159	$134	$165	33%
	Second Year New Donors (New Donors Last Year)				
Number—Beginning of Year	2,993	2,731	1,916	2,095	–30%
Number Renewing This Year	828	688	612	767	–7%
Percent Renewing This Year	28%	25%	32%	37%	32%
Number of Gifts	2,962	2,096	2,198	2,510	–15%
Value of Gifts	$217,173	$180,313	$250,548	$210,400	–3%
Avg. # of Gifts/Donor	3.6	3.0	3.6	3.3	–9%
Average Gift Size	$73	$86	$114	$84	14%
Annual Giving/Donor	$262	$262	$409	$274	5%

TABLE D.3 Fundraising Overview Report, Cont'd.

Donor Status Beginning of Year	1996	1997	1998	1999	% Change '96–'99
Multi-Year Donors (Gave Last 2+ Years)					
Number—Beginning of Year	0	10,501	9,811	9,230	-12%
Number Renewing This Year	0	8,475	8,066	7,470	-12%
Percent Renewing This Year	0%	81%	82%	81%	0%
Number of Gifts	0	43,522	41,026	38,678	-11%
Value of Gifts	$0	$3,642,265	$3,668,948	$3,642,792	0%
Avg. # of Gifts/Donor	0.0	5.1	5.1	5.2	1%
Average Gift Size	$0	$84	$89	$94	13%
Annual Giving/Donor	$0	$430	$455	$488	13%
Lapsed Donors (No Gift Last Year, Given Previously)					
Number—Beginning of Year	2,171	5,945	9,763	12,311	467%
Number Renewing This Year	1,577	1,188	1,144	1,174	-26%
Percent Renewing This Year	0%	15%	15%	19%	22%
Number of Gifts	2,424	1,845	1,771	1,774	-27%
Value of Gifts	$222,961	$214,585	$210,618	$260,728	17%
Avg. # of Gifts/Donor	1.5	1.6	1.5	1.5	-2%
Average Gift Size	$92	$116	$119	$147	60%
Annual Giving/Donor	$141	$181	$184	$222	57%

Second Year Reactivated Donors (Lapsed Donors, Reactivated Last Year)

Number—Beginning of Year	12,847	1,577	1,188	1,144	−91%
Number Renewing This Year	9,673	648	552	536	−94%
Percent Renewing This Year	75%	41%	46%	47%	−38%
Number of Gifts	46,877	1,457	1,175	1,139	−98%
Value of Gifts	$3,706,541	$134,672	$143,117	$128,732	−97%
Avg. # of Gifts/Donor	4.8	2.2	2.1	2.1	−56%
Average Gift Size	$79	$92	$122	$113	43%
Annual Giving/Donor	$383	$208	$259	$240	−37%

Totals: All Donor Types

Number Giving This Year	14,809	12,915	12,469	12,168	−18%
Number of Gifts	56,136	51,883	49,273	47,826	−15%
Value of Gifts	$4,484,866	$4,476,962	$4,554,557	$4,608,699	3%
Avg. # of Gifts/Donor	3.8	4.0	4.0	3.9	4%
Average Gift Size	$80	$86	$92	$96	21%
Annual Giving/Donor	$303	$347	$365	$379	25%

donors and those who have given infrequently. Then they must decide how to best develop these segments. There are several ways to conduct this analysis. The most simple is to run a number of frequency analyses and have an expert design the segmentation subjectively, based on the analyses and his experience and understanding of nonprofit direct marketing. More sophisticated means employ statistical techniques such as CHAID, CART, clustering algorithms, and multiple regression (see Resource B).

Response Modeling

Sometimes a direct-marketing oriented nonprofit wants to learn how to find the best prospects in a database, whether its own or another's. To find these prospects, an analysis is performed that compares the database characteristics of those who donated to the nonprofit with the characteristics of those who did not. The nondonors may be profiled in the nonprofit's database or an outside database. Having identified the ideal characteristics, the organization analyzes the prospect database. In this process, a *score* is placed in each person's record indicating the likelihood that she will donate. Because this form of analysis isn't yet very exact, the scores are often in the form of deciles, in other words, 1 through 10. A score of 1 marks those most likely to donate, and 10 marks those least likely to donate. A calculation of the expected value of an acquisition mailing to each decile can be used to determine how many pieces should be mailed. Often, logistic regression is used for response analysis.

Resource E: Organizations Helpful to Nonprofit Researchers

Survey Software

The Survey System

Creative Research Systems

411 B Street, Suite 2

Petaluma, CA 94952-3057

Telephone: 707-765-1001

Fax: 707-765-1068

E-mail: surveys@wco.com

Internet: www.surveysystem.com

The Survey System is a good, economical CATI (computer assisted telephone interviewing) software system. The base package costs only about $500. Additional interviewing stations and many optional modules are available at additional cost.

Stat-Pac

Stat-Pac Inc.

4425 Thomas Avenue, South

Minneapolis, MN 55410

Telephone: 612-925-0159

Fax: 612-925-0851

E-mail: admin.statpac.com

Internet: www.statpac.com

Stat-PacIV Gold is a system that has been well used by thousands of organizations. Currently available for DOS and Windows, it has pull-down menus, does a great job of allowing the user to design questionnaires, and is especially strong in terms of statistical analysis. It is user friendly, comprehensive, and dependable.

SPSS, Inc.

SPSS, Inc.

233 S. Wacker, 11th Floor

Chicago, IL 60606-6307

Telephone: 312-651-3000

Fax: 312-651-3444

E-mail: spss.com

Internet: www.spss.com

SPSS, Inc. is excellent general statistical software. It can be used for surveys as well as most other kinds of statistical applications. It is offered for mainframes as well as for PCs.

Professional Research Associations

Marketing Research Association

Marketing Research Association

1344 Silas Deane Highway, Suite 300

Rocky Hill, CT 06067

Telephone: 860-257-4008

Fax: 860-257-3990

E-mail: mra-net.org

Internet: www.mra-net.org

Council for the Advancement of Survey Research Organizations (CASRO)

CASRO

3 Upper Devon

Port Jefferson, NY 11777

Telephone: 631-928-6954

Fax: 631-928-6041

E-mail: casro@casro.org

Internet: www.casro.org

Directories of Focus Group Field Centers and Other Research Companies

The Blue Book

c/o Marketing Research Association

1344 Silas Deane Highway, Suite 300

Rocky Hill, CT 06067

Telephone: 860-257-4008

Fax: 860-257-3990

E-mail: mra-net.org

Internet: www.bluebook.org

The Blue Book lists many research organizations throughout the country and is especially strong in its listings of focus groups facilities.

The Green Book

c/o American Marketing Association—New York

New York AMA

The Lincoln Building

60 East 42nd Street

New York, NY 10165

Telephone: 212-687-3280

Fax: 212-557-9242

E-mail: ccrifasi@nyama.org

Internet: www.greenbook.org

The Green Book lists many research organizations throughout country.

Quirk's Marketing Research Review

Quirk's Marketing Research Review

8030 Cedar Avenue South, Suite 229

Minneapolis, MN 55425

Telephone: 612-854-5101

Fax: 612-854-8191

E-mail: info@quirks.com

Internet: www.quirks.com

Quirk's Marketing Research Review is a great research industry publication. It has lots of articles about how to improve survey, focus group and other forms of research. In addition, each issue has a special theme, such as annual directories of research firms, focus group facilities, data processing software manufacturers, data processing vendors, etc.

Index

A

Actionable data, defined, 155
Advanced survey analysis tools, 161–165
Appendices, in survey report, 145-146

B

Banners analysis, 128-129
Banners points, 128-129
Bar graphs, 133-134
Battery of questions, 73-75, 96, 116; defined, 155
Bias: rotation of questions and, 66; in survey questions, 57-60, 72
Bleed effect, defined, 155
Blind survey, 81, 94; defined, 51
Budgeting, 29-30

C

Callback prompting, 115
CATI (computer-assisted telephone interviewing), 52, 66, 122-123; advantages of, 114-117; defined, 155-156; vendor list, 117
Census, defined, 12-13
Chi-square test, 130
Cluster analysis, segmentation and, 173
Communication, nonprofit-constituent, 11. *See also* Feedback
Comprehensive surveys, primary objective of, 31

Computer-assisted personal interviewing (CAPI), 20
Conclusions, in survey report, 143
Confidence interval: defined, 43; and frequency analysis, 124-126
Confidence level, 43-44
Confidentiality, 110
Constituent bonding, 31
Constituent file audit, 202
Constituent groups: identification and prioritization of, 29; survey objectives and, 31
Constituent importance modeling, 162, 174-178
Constituent-initiated feedback, 12
Cooperation rate, defined, 156
Cross-tabulation analysis, 97, 126-128

D

Data analysis techniques, in direct marketing, 193-197
Database packages, 123-124
Demographics: defined, 156; in questionnaire design, 55, 96
Depth (one-on-one) interview: advantages and disadvantages of, 16, 191-192; defined, 156
Difference of means test, 130
Difference of proportions test, 130
Donor file audit, 202
Donor survey. *See* Survey research

E

Estimate of error. *See* Confidence interval
Executive summary, in survey report, 146-148

F

Factorial analysis, and direct-mail testing, 193-197
Feasibility studies, 192
Feedback: nonverbal, 17; qualitative, 14-17; quantitative 12-14; verbal, 11-17
Focus groups, 17, 187-191; advantages and disadvantages of, 15-16; defined, 15; facilities for conducting, 15; as qualitative research, 188; screening questions and, 50-51
Frequency analysis, 124-126; recoding and, 126

G

General population, defined, 39-40
Graphic analysis: basic tools in, 132-135; value of, 132

I

Importance modeling, 162, 174-178
Incentives, 53-54
In-house research: advantages of, 179-180; costs of, 22
In-person interview: advantages and disadvantages, 16, 191-192; computer-assisted (CAPI), 20; costs, 120-121; effectiveness of, 36; guidelines, 120; ideal length for, 57
Internet survey, 37; validity of, 121
Interval scale, defined, 157
Interviews: evaluation and monitoring of, 116, 119; open-ended questions in, 14-15. *See also* In-person interview; Telephone survey interviewer
Introduction, in survey report, 143-145

L

Lifetime value analysis, 197-202
Likert Scale, 96; defined, 157
Line graphs, 134

M

Magazine enclosures, 35
Mail survey: alphabetized items in, 67; answer rotation in, 66; and blind surveys, 94; cover letter, 52, 109-110; graphic design of, 97; ideal length for, 56; implementation of, 109-114; independent, 37; introduction in, 108; for membership organizations, example of, 97-108; pretest, 69; and response coding, 108; sample, 97-108; screening questions in, 50; subgroup tracking strategy in, 113-114
Mailing lists, evaluation of, 200
Major donor screening, 161, 162-165
Major donor survey, primary objective of, 31
Mean, defined, 130
Median, defined, 130-131
Member bonding, 31
Member survey, 31
Membership organizations, questionnaire design for, 97
Microsoft Excel, 123, 131
Missing cases, 124
Mode, defined, 131

N

Newsletter enclosures, 35
Nonprobability techniques, 42-43
Nth name select, 41
Numeric questions, analysis of, 130-131

O

One-on-one interview. *See* Depth interview
Open-ended questions: advantages and disadvantages of, 61-62; analysis of responses to, 131-132; defined, 158
Ordinal scale: defined, 158; Likert scale and, 96, 157
Organization-initiated feedback, 12-14

P

Perceptual mapping, 162, 165-171
Pie graphs, 132
Population, defined, 39-40
Priority-setting, and market research, 8

Probability sampling techniques, 40-42
Problem-solving, use of research for, 8
Professional research associations, 208-209
Professional researcher, 189; advantages of, 180-182; confidentiality and, 110, 112-113; costs of, 22, 185; selection of, 182-184
Program effectiveness survey, 3
Prospect search, 192-193
Prospect survey, primary objective of, 31
Psychographics, defined, 158

Q

Qualified prospect screening, 161, 162-165
Qualitative research: advanced, 187-192; versus quantitative, 17; timing of, 16-17; types of, 15-16; usefulness of, 14-15
Quantitative research: key factors in, 13; timing of, 16-17; usefulness of, 13-14
Question(s): battery, 73-75, 96, 116; closed-ended, advantages of, 62; demographic, 55, 96; dual-issue, 58-59; formatting, 60-67, 71-80; initial, 94; interval-scale, 65; key word/concept in, 71; minimizing bias in, 72; multiple-choice, 64; open-ended, advantages and disadvantages of, 61-62; ordinal scale responses to, 64-65; "other" and "don't know" option in, 60, 62; placement of, 55; response option order in, 65-66; rotation of, 66, 116; superfluous, 57; unprompted, 63. *See also* Response options
Questionnaire design, 49-69; basic principles of, 49; introduction in, 51-53, 93; language in, 58; length in, 52-53, 56-57; minimizing bias in, 57-60; objectivity in, 58; of outer envelope, 111-112; presentation of, 110-111; pretest and approval of, 67-69; of reply envelope, 112-113; and response rate, 51-57; screening questions in, 49-51; sequencing and flow in, 55-56, 95-96. *See also* Mail survey; Telephone survey

R

Random sampling, 40-42
Range of error. *See* Confidence interval

Readership survey, primary objective of, 31-32
Research firm. *See* Professional researcher
Research objectives, 28; primary, 30-31; secondary, 32-33
Research quality, response rate and, 33-34
Research tools, 187-206; direct marketing data analysis as, 193-206; qualitative, 187-192; traditional, 192-193. *See also* Survey methodology
Response analysis, in direct marketing, 206
Response differences, analysis of, 129-130
Response options: categorical, 75-76; continuum, 75-79; rotation of, 116; simple, 75; types of, 96
Response rate, 13; defined, 34; means for increasing, 35; and survey's quality, 33-34; techniques for maximizing, 51-57

S

Sample: defined, 13; representativeness, 13
Sample size, 13; selection of, 43-47, 126; and subgroups, 47-48
Sampling: frame, defined, 39-40; population, 39-40; quotas, computer-assisted tracking of, 115; statistics, in written report, 139; techniques, 40-43
Scandals, and donor skepticism, 6
Segmentation, 162, 171-174; demographic versus behavioral measures in, 172-173; in direct marketing, 202-206
Self-selected minority, 13
Skip patterns, and computer-assisted interviewing, 114-117
Software, 122-124, 207-208; complexity of, 123; personal interview and, 20. *See also* CATI (computer-assisted telephone interviewing)
Spreadsheet packages, 123
SPSS (Statistical Package for the Social Sciences), 123
SPSS, Inc., 208
Stacked bar graphs, 134
Statistical analyses: overview of, 124-129; and true difference versus coincidental difference, 129-130
Statistically significant differences, 130
Stat-Pak, 122, 207-208
Stratified random sampling, 41-42
Stubs, defined, 128

Subgroup tracking, 113-114, 115
Subquestions, 72-75; rotation of, 116
Subsampling, 47-48
Survey analysis, 122-135; and data entry, 124; graphic, 132-134; software for, 122-124; statistical, 124-132. *See also* Advanced survey analysis tools
Survey costs: budgeting and, 29-30; in-house, 22; of outside researcher, 22
Survey design, 20, 28-48; case studies, 1-7; qualitative research and, 15; as quantitative research, 13; sampling in, 38-48. *See also* Questionnaire design
Survey methodology: combined method in, 38; comparative, 35-38; enclosed with appeal, 36; enclosed with magazine/newsletter, 35; in-person, 36; Internet-based, 37; and survey report, 138-139. *See also* Mail survey; Telephone survey
Survey report, 139-142; audience for, 136; formatting of, 150; preparation, 136-150; and prior research, 138; section-by-section guidelines, 138-149; table of contents in, 150; writing order, 137
Survey research: case studies, 1-7; as quantitative research, 13; resistance to, 30; value of, 8-9
Survey System, 122-123, 207

Sweepstakes appeals, 6-7
Systematic random sampling, 40, 41, 43

T

Target population, screening for, 49-51
Telephone survey, 81-97; costs of, 38; effectiveness of, 37-38; ideal length for, 56; implementation of, 114-117; pretest, 69; rotation of questions and responses in, 66-67; sample, 82-93; screening questions in, 50. *See also* CATI (computer-assisted telephone interviewing)
Telephone survey interviewer: monitoring of, 119; motivation strategies, 119-120; performance evaluation, 116; selection and training, 117-119; telemarketing experience and, 117
Title page, in survey report, 146

U

Universe, defined, 39

W

White space, defined, 159
Working population, defined, 39-40